Alastair
Sawday's

Special Places
to Stay

British
Bed & Breakfast

"The best-selling guide to
British B&Bs... nothing quite
compares."
The Bookseller

ipa
Environmental
award winner 2005

Edited by Nicola Crosse

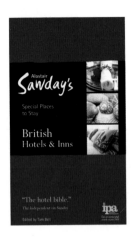

Alastair
Sawday's

Special Places
to Stay

British
Hotels & Inns

"The hotel bible."
The Independent on Sunday

ipa

Edited by Tom Bell

Alastair
Sawday's

Special Places
to Stay

Devon &
Cornwall

"When they say 'special'
that's exactly what you get."
Glamour

Edited by Nicola Crosse

Alastair
Sawday's

Special Places
to Stay

Scotland

"Much-loved guidebooks."
The Guardian

ipa
Environmental
award winner 2005

Alastair
Sawday's

Special Places to Stay

Fifth edition
Copyright © 2009 Alastair Sawday
Publishing Co. Ltd
Published in 2009
ISBN-13: 978-1-906136-10-9

Alastair Sawday Publishing Co. Ltd,
The Old Farmyard, Yanley Lane,
Long Ashton, Bristol BS41 9LR, UK
Tel: +44 (0)1275 395430
Email: info@sawdays.co.uk
Web: www.sawdays.co.uk

The Globe Pequot Press,
P. O. Box 480, Guilford,
Connecticut 06437, USA
Tel: +1 203 458 4500
Email: info@globepequot.com
Web: www.globepequot.com

Series Editor Alastair Sawday
Editor Nicola Crosse
Assistant to Editor Wendy Ogden
Editorial Director Annie Shillito
Writing Nicola Crosse
Inspections Jan Adams, David Ashby,
Neil Brown, Angie Collings,
Vickie MacIver, Scott Reeve,
Aideen Reid, Mandy Wragg
And thanks to those people who did an
inspection or two!
Accounts Bridget Bishop,
Shona Adcock
Editorial Sue Bourner,
Jo Boissevain, Claire Wilson
Production Julia Richardson,
Rachel Coe, Tom Germain,
Anny Mortada
Sales & Marketing & PR
Rob Richardson,
Sarah Bolton, Bethan Riach
Web & IT Joe Green,
Chris Banks, Phil Clarke, Mike Peake,
Russell Wilkinson

Maps: Maidenhead Cartographic Services
Printing: Butler, Tanner & Dennis, Frome
UK distribution: Penguin UK, London

Alastair Sawday's

Special Places to Stay

British Bed & Breakfast
for Garden Lovers

4 Contents

The buildings

Beautiful as they were, our old offices leaked heat, used electricity to heat water and rooms, flooded spaces with light to illuminate one person, and were not ours to alter.

So in 2005 we created our own eco-offices by converting some old barns to create a low-emissions building. Heating and lighting the building, which houses over 30 employees, now produces only 0.28 tonnes of carbon dioxide per year. Not bad when you compare this with the 6 tonnes emitted by the average UK household. We achieved this through a variety of innovative and energy-saving building techniques, described below.

Insulation   We went to great lengths to ensure that very little heat will escape, by:
- laying insulating board 90mm thick immediately under the roof tiles and on the floor
- lining the whole of the inside of the building with plastic sheeting to ensure air-tightness
- fixing further insulation underneath the roof and between the rafters
- fixing insulated plaster-board to add another layer of insulation.

All this means we are insulated for the Arctic, and almost totally air-tight.

Heating   We installed a wood-pellet boiler from Austria, in order to be largely fossil-fuel free. The pellets are made from compressed sawdust, a waste product from timber mills that work only with sustainably managed forests. The heat is conveyed by water to all corners of the building via an under-floor system.

Water   We installed a 6000-litre tank to collect rainwater from the roofs. This is pumped back, via an ultra-violet filter, to the lavatories, showers and basins. There are two solar thermal panels on the roof providing heat to the one (massively insulated) hot-water cylinder.

Lighting   We have a carefully planned mix of low-energy lighting: task lighting and up-lighting. We also installed three sun-pipes – polished aluminium tubes that reflect the outside light down to chosen areas of the building.

Electricity   All our electricity has long come from the Good Energy Company and is 100% renewable.

Materials   Virtually all materials are non-toxic or natural. Our carpets, for example, are made from (80%) Herdwick sheep-wool from National Trust farms in the Lake District.

Doors and windows   Outside doors and new windows are wooden, double-glazed, beautifully constructed in Norway. Old windows have been double-glazed.

We have a building we are proud of, and architects and designers are fascinated by. But best of all, we are now in a better position to encourage our owners and readers to take sustainability more seriously.

Photo: Tom Germain

What we do

Besides moving the business to a low-carbon building, the company works in a number of ways to reduce its overall environmental footprint:

- all office travel is logged as part of a carbon sequestration programme, and money for compensatory tree-planting is dispatched to SCAD in India for a tree-planting and development project
- we avoid flying and take the train for business trips wherever possible; when we have to fly, we 'double offset'
- car-sharing and the use of a company pool car are part of company policy; recycled cooking oil is used in one car and LPG in the other
- organic and Fair Trade basic provisions are used in the staff kitchen and organic food is provided by the company at all in-house events
- green cleaning products are used throughout the office
- all kitchen waste is composted and used on the office organic allotment.

Our total 'operational' carbon footprint (including travel to and from work, plus all our trips to visit our Special Places to Stay) is just over 17 tonnes per year. We have come a long way, but we would like to get this figure as close to zero as possible.

For many years Alastair Sawday Publishing has been 'greening' the business in different ways. Our aim is to reduce our environmental footprint as far as possible – with almost everything we do we have the environmental implications in mind. (We once claimed to be the world's first carbon-neutral publishing company, but are now wary of such claims.) In recognition of our efforts we won a Business Commitment to the Environment Award in 2005, and in 2006 a Queen's Award for Enterprise in the Sustainable Development category. In that year Alastair was voted ITN's 'Eco Hero'.

We have created our own eco-offices by converting former barns to create a low-emissions building. Through a variety of innovative and energy-saving techniques this has reduced our carbon emissions by 35%.

Photo: Tom Germain

But becoming 'green' is a journey and, although we began long before most companies, we still have a long way to go.

In 2008 we won the Independent Publishers Guild Environmental Award. The judging panel were effusive in their praise, stating: "With green issues currently at the forefront of publishers' minds, Alastair Sawday Publishing was singled out in this category as a model for all independents to follow. Its efforts to reduce waste in its office and supply chain have reduced the company's environmental impact, and it works closely with staff to identify more areas of improvement. Here is a publisher who lives and breathes green. Alastair Sawday has all the right principles and is clearly committed to improving its practice further."

Our Fragile Earth series is a growing collection of campaigning books about the environment. Highlighting the perilous state of the world yet offering imaginative and radical solutions and some intriguing facts, these books will make you weep and smile. They will keep you up to date and well armed for the battle with apathy.

THE QUEEN'S AWARDS
FOR ENTERPRISE:
SUSTAINABLE DEVELOPMENT
2006

I have boundless admiration for gardeners. They possess ancient knowledge, responding to the whims and skills of Mother Nature with their own. That there are millions of them in this country only reinforces my admiration, and sense of inadequacy.

I am often struck by the generosity of gardeners, their willingness to give plants, cuttings, advice and moral support. It is curious how mere mortals should be so impelled to generosity and neighbourliness by their gardens. There is hope for us all as the credit crunch forces more of us to pick up our spades. We may learn to give and take, get our hands dirty and take pleasure from simple things.

Food security is much on my mind as I write this – energy security too, and our vulnerability to rising prices. But we need food more than we need oil. We need massively to increase the amount of land given over to gardening and small-holding. The skills and imagination employed by the people in this book will be much in demand. It is satisfying that more and more of them are growing vegetables as well as flowers and plants.

Twenty-four gardens in this edition are open for the National Gardens Scheme or its Scottish cousin. Nine are in the Good Gardens guide and many are RHS associates, or are involved in creating National Collections. A new garden to this book, in County Durham, holds the

National Plant Collections of Gilia, Polemonium and Hakonechloa. Another new one, in Norfolk, holds the National Plant Collection of Miscanthus.

There are important gardens here, and some arty ones too. Not all of them are huge; there are some new town gardens and hidden gems, a trend likely to continue as available space shrinks. But there is one trend which especially warms my heart: encouraging you to linger all day. Here are over 60 places to stay where you don't have to leave right after breakfast!

Alastair Sawday

The poor gardener! When I wrote the introduction to the last edition of this book we had just been through two of the hottest summers anyone could remember, hosepipe bans were in place in the South East of the country and grass was turning brown all over the land — even in Northumberland! Over the phone I heard miserable stories of ruined herbaceous borders, flopping flowers, cracks in the soil and trip after trip into gardens carrying bath water to try and save things in pots. Those who planned NGS open afternoons were most anxious, and not surprisingly, as all that hard work in the winter and early spring was about not to pay off. The newspapers were filled with pictures of people standing beside dried up river and stream beds, reservoirs were at their lowest levels for years. We were all urged to save water while the water companies paid their highest executives huge salaries and bonuses.

Two years ago several of the owners in this book had already decided that global warming would mean they would almost definitely have to alter the way they gardened, magazines were filled with examples of the Mediterranean garden, pebbles and stones enjoyed a revival in nurseries, as did grasses, herbs and succulents. Decking was still popular, and masses of stone paving — swathes of lawns and pots of annuals discouraged as being just too water-hungry. But even with all these things in place the gardener was not home and dry in any sense. Just as soon as we had devised the perfect, practically drought-proof, maintenance-free garden of the twenty first century, global warming took a different turn.

The last two summers were the wettest I can remember. The lovely tall grasses at work were flattened in July and August by torrential rain — the lavenders flowered perfectly then the flowers rotted on their stems, tomatoes without a greenhouse have not ripened and produce from the allotment has been scanty — apart from potatoes and runner beans — mainly because it was just too foul to work on it in the rain. Some owners have had disasters with taller plants like delphiniums and lupins, roses did not have a good year generally and spring and summer flooding has wrought havoc in many counties.

Some environmentalists blame flooding, in part, on too much decking and concrete in people's gardens, apparently there is

nowhere for the water to run. And the Slow Food movement is encouraging us all to dig up our flower beds anyway, and plant vegetables instead. If we have no garden then we are urged to grow strawberries and lettuces in pots on our window sills. Self-sufficiency is trumpeted as the way forward.

So where does all this leave the poor, confused gardener? I cannot speak for all, but the owners in this book have been brilliant at keeping apace, riding the storm, predicting what may happen and dealing with it. The true gardener is not just a horny handed man or woman of the soil. He or she is an artist and their creative juices flow as easily when it is raining as when the sun is shining. Just as the writer will scribble on anything to hand when they have no proper paper, and the painter will use and re-use old canvasses to get his ideas down, the true gardener will manage to create something beautiful whatever the weather throws at them and however many plants get damaged in the process.

There are wonderful examples of true artistry in this book, some of these gardens are old favourites and others are new to us. Some are quirky with humorous topiary and giant sculptures, some concentrate on just a few National Plant Collections. There are tiny town gardens, pretty cottage gardens and some rather grand ones that are also open to the public, so it's a huge treat to stay the night and have another wander round in the morning. And vegetable growing does appear to be on the increase: allotment waiting lists are lengthening, sales of veg seeds and fruit trees are increasing. The majority of owners in this book grow their own vegetables and soft fruit, much of which ends up on your plate. From the wilds of northern Scotland to the balmy fringes of Cornwall and Devon, via some Welsh glories and everything in between, there are many absolute stunners here for you to explore. I hope that whichever place you choose to stay you will find there some inspiration and ideas to try out yourselves. Talk to the owners, they are a source of deep knowledge, and they nearly always like to talk about their best subject!

I do hope you enjoy using this book and meeting a few of the army of artists who work so hard to keep the gardens in this book at their absolute best. It is comforting to know that they are there, preserving what is our heritage – the British garden.

Nicola Crosse

Photo left: Tregoose, entry 14

It's simple. There are no rules, no boxes to tick. We choose places that we like and are fiercely subjective in our choices. We also recognise that one person's idea of special is not necessarily someone else's so there is a huge variety of places, and prices, in the book. Those who are familiar with our Special Places series know that we look for comfort, originality, authenticity, and reject the insincere, the anonymous and the banal. The way guests are treated comes as high on our list as the setting, the architecture, the atmosphere and the food.

Inspections

We visit every place in the guide to get a feel for how both house and owner tick. We don't take a clipboard and we don't have a list of what is acceptable and what is not. Instead, we chat for an hour or so with the owner and look round. It's all very informal, but it gives us an excellent idea of who would enjoy staying there. If the visit happens to be the last of the day, we sometimes stay the night. Once in the book, properties are re-inspected every three to four years so that we can keep things fresh and accurate.

Feedback

In between inspections we rely on feedback from our army of readers, as well as from staff members who are encouraged to visit properties across the series. This feedback is invaluable to us and we always follow up on comments.

Photo: Pennard House, entry 75

So do tell us whether your stay has been a joy or not, if the atmosphere was great or stuffy, the owners cheery or bored. The accuracy of the book depends on what you, and our inspectors, tell us. A lot of the new entries in each edition are recommended by our readers, so keep telling us about new places you've discovered too. Please use the forms on our website at www.sawdays.co.uk, or later in this book (page 301).

However, please do not tell us if the bedside light was broken, or the shower head was scummy. Tell the owner, immediately, and get them to do something about it. Most owners are more than happy to correct problems and will bend over backwards to help. Far better than bottling it up and then writing to us a week later!

Subscriptions

Owners pay to appear in this guide. Their fee goes towards the high costs of inspecting, of producing an all-colour book and of maintaining our website. We only include places that we like and find special for one reason or another, so it is not possible for anyone to buy their way onto these pages. Nor is it possible for the owner to write their own description. We will say if the bedrooms are small, or if a main road is near. We do our best to avoid misleading people.

Disclaimer

We make no claims to pure objectivity in choosing these places. They are here simply because we like them. Our opinions and tastes are ours alone and this book is a statement of them; we hope you will share them. We have done our utmost to get our facts right but apologise unreservedly for any mistakes that may have crept in.

You should know that we don't check such things as fire regulations, swimming pool security or any other laws with which owners of properties receiving paying guests should comply. This is the responsibility of the owners.

Photo above: Whitehouse Farm Cottage, entry 3
Photo right: Millgate House, entry 104

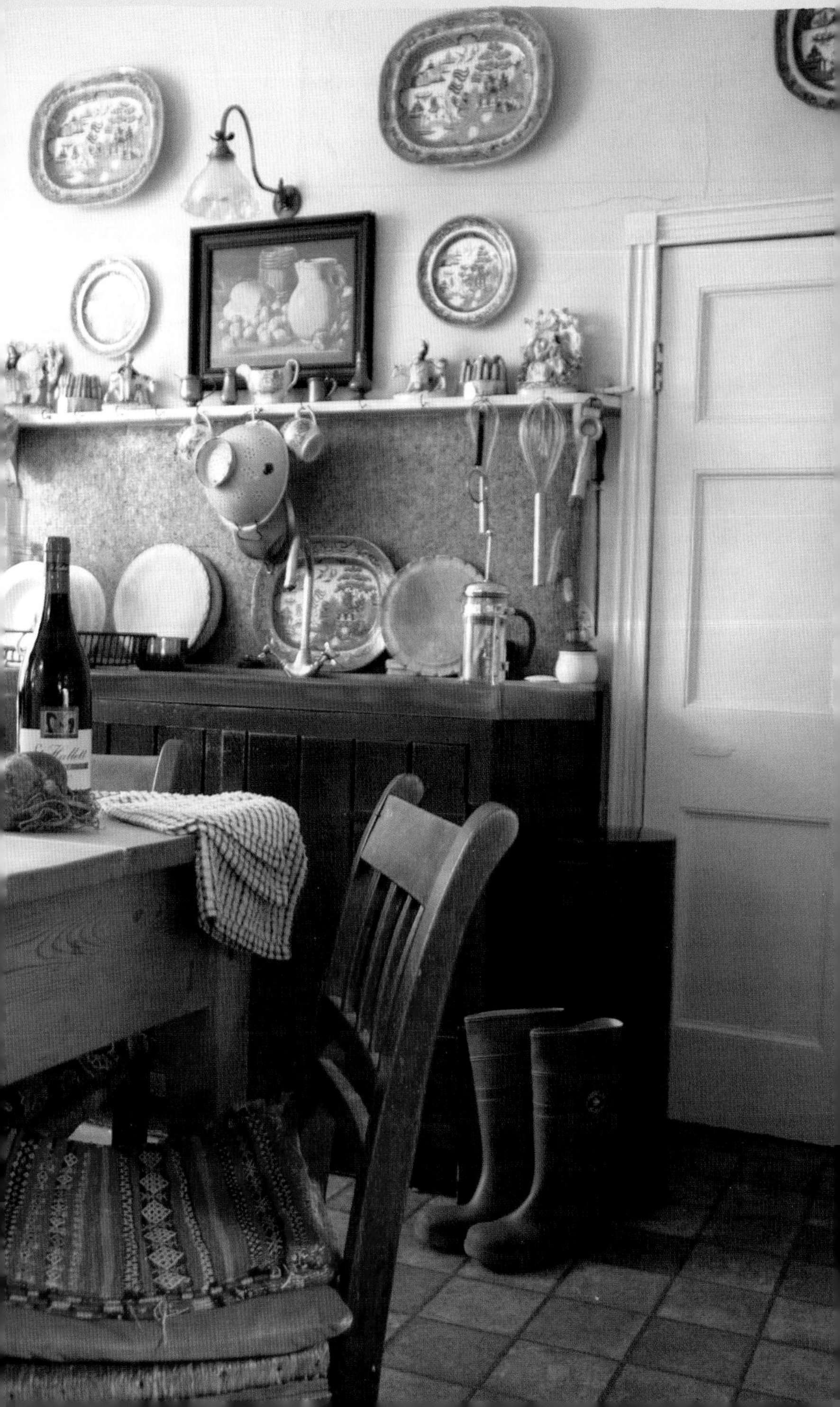

Finding the right place for you

All these places are special in one way or another. All have been visited and then written about honestly so that you can take what you like and leave the rest. Those of you who swear by Sawday's books trust our write-ups precisely because we don't have a blanket standard; we include places simply because we like them. But we all have different priorities, so do read and choose carefully.

Our descriptions are carefully composed to help you steer clear of places that will not suit you, but instead lead you to personal paradise. If something is particularly important to you then do check when you book: a simple question or two can avoid misunderstandings.

Maps

Each property is flagged with its entry number on the maps at the front. These maps are a great starting point for planning your trip, but please don't use them as anything other than a general guide – use a decent road map for real navigation. Most places will send you detailed instructions once you have booked your stay.

Ethical Collection

We're always keen to draw attention to owners who are striving to have a positive impact on the world, so you'll notice that some entries are flagged as being part of our "Ethical Collection". These places are working hard to reduce their environmental footprint, making significant contributions to their local community, or are passionate about serving local or organic food. Owners have had to fill in a very detailed questionnaire before becoming part of this Collection – read more on page 294. This doesn't mean that other places in the guide are not taking similar initiatives – many are – but we may not yet know about them.

Sawday's Travel Club

We've recently launched a Travel Club, based around the Special Places to Stay series; you'll see a 🧳 symbol on those places offering something extra to Club members, so to find out how to join see page 290.

Symbols

Below each entry you will see some symbols, which are explained at the very back of the book. They are based on the information given to us by the owners. However, things do change: bikes may be

Photo: South Lodge, entry 5

under repair or a new pool may have been put in. Please use the symbols as a guide rather than an absolute statement of fact and double-check anything that is important to you — owners occasionally bend their own rules, so it's worth asking if you may take your child or dog even if they don't have the symbol.

Children — The ♀ symbol shows places which are happy to accept children of all ages. This does not mean that they will necessarily have cots, high chairs, etc. If an owner welcomes children but only those above a certain age, we have put these details at the end of their write-up. These houses do not have the child symbol, but even these folk may accept your younger child if you are the only guests. Many who say no to children do so not because they don't like them but because they may have a steep stair, an unfenced pond or they find balancing the needs of mixed age groups too challenging.

Pets — Our 🐾 symbol shows places which are happy to accept pets. It means they can sleep in the bedroom with you, but not on the bed. Be realistic about your pet — if it is nervous or excitable or doesn't like the company of other dogs, people, chickens, or children, then say so.

Owners' pets — The 🐈 symbol is given when the owners have their own pet on the premises. It may not be a cat! But it is there to warn you that you may be greeted by a dog, serenaded by a parrot, or indeed sat upon by a cat.

Photo: Tremayne House, entry 11

Quick reference indices

At the back of the book you'll find a number of quick-reference indices showing those places that offer a particular service, perhaps a room for under £70 a night, or owners who are happy for you to stay all day. They are worth flicking through if you are looking for something specific.

A further listing refers to houses within two miles of a Sustrans National Cycle Network route. Take your own bike or check if you can hire or borrow one from the owners before you travel, and enjoy a cycle ride on your break.

Types of places

Some houses have rooms in annexes or stables, barns or garden 'wings', some of which feel part of the house, some of which don't. If you have a strong preference for being in the throng or for being apart, check those details. Consider your surroundings when you are packing: large, ancient country houses may be cooler than you are used to; city places and working farms may be noisy at times; and that peacock or cockerel we mention may disturb you. Light sleepers should pack ear plugs, and take a dressing gown if there's a separate bathroom (though these are sometimes provided).

Some owners give you a front door key so you may come and go as you please; others like to have the house empty between, say, 10am and 4pm. If you would prefer not to wander far during the day then look for the places that have the 'Stay all day' quick reference at the back of the book.

Rooms

Bedrooms — We tell you if a room is a double, twin/double (ie with zip and link beds), suite (with a sitting area), family or single. Most owners are flexible and can juggle beds or bedrooms; talk to them about what you need before you book. It is rare to be given your own room key in a B&B.

Bathrooms — Most bedrooms in this book have an en suite bath or shower room; we only mention bathroom details when they do not. So, you may get a 'separate' bathroom (yours alone but not in your room) or a shared bathroom. Under certain entries we mention that two rooms share a bathroom and are 'let to same party only'. Please do not assume this means you must be a group of friends to apply; it simply means that if you book one of these rooms you will not be sharing a bathroom with strangers. If these things are important to you, please check when booking. Bath/shower means a bath with shower over; bath and shower means there is a separate shower unit.

Sitting rooms — Most B&B owners offer guests the family sitting room to share, or they provide a sitting room specially for guests. If neither option is available we generally say so, but do check. And do not assume that every bedroom or sitting room has a TV.

Meals

Unless we say otherwise, a full cooked breakfast is included. Some owners will give you a good continental breakfast instead. Often you will feast on local sausage and bacon, eggs from resident hens, homemade breads and jams. In some you may have organic yogurts and beautifully presented fruit compotes. Some owners are fairly unbending about breakfast times, others are happy to just wait until you want it, or even bring it to you in bed.

Apart from breakfast, no meals should be expected unless you have arranged them in advance. Although we don't say so on each entry – the repetition would be tedious – all owners who provide packed lunch, lunch or dinner need ADVANCE NOTICE. And they want to get things right for you so, when booking, please discuss your diet and meal times. Meal prices are quoted per person, and dinner is often a social occasion shared with your hosts and other guests.

Do eat in if you can – this book is teeming with good cooks. And how much more relaxing after a day out to have to move no further than the dining room for an excellent dinner, and to eat and drink knowing there's only a flight of stairs between you and your bed. Very few of our houses are licensed, but most are happy for you to bring your own drink.

Photo: Winforton Court, entry 41

Prices and minimum stays

Each entry gives a price PER ROOM for two people. We also include prices for single rooms, and let you know if there is a supplement to pay should you choose to loll in a double bed on your own.

The price range for each B&B covers a one-night stay in the cheapest room in low season to the most expensive in high season. Some owners charge more at certain times (during regattas or festivals, for example) and some charge less for stays of more than one night. Some

owners ask for a two-night minimum stay at weekends and we mention this where possible. Most of our houses could fill many times over on peak weekends and during the summer; book early, especially if you have specific needs.

Booking and cancellation

Do be clear about the room booked and the price for B&B and for meals. Requests for deposits vary; some are non-refundable, and some owners may charge you for the whole of the booked stay in advance.

Some cancellation policies are more stringent than others. It is also worth noting that some owners will take this deposit directly from your credit/debit card without contacting you to discuss it. So ask them to explain their cancellation policy clearly before booking so you understand exactly where you stand; it may well avoid a nasty surprise.

Payment

All our owners take cash and UK cheques with a cheque card. Few take credit cards but if they do, we have given them the appropriate symbol. Check that your particular credit card is acceptable.

Tipping

Owners do not expect tips. If you have been treated with extraordinary kindness, write to them, or leave a small gift. Please tell us, too – we love to hear, and we do note, all feedback.

Arrivals and departures

Say roughly what time you will arrive (normally after 4pm), as most hosts like to welcome you personally. Be on time if you have booked dinner; if, despite best efforts, you are delayed, phone to give warning.

Closed

When given in months this means the whole of the month stated.

Smoking

The majority of places do not allow smoking anywhere on the property; if they do, we have added a note to the end of their write up.

Photo: Hall End House, entry 45

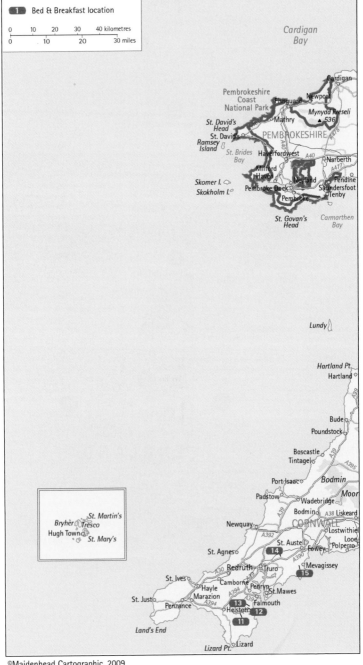

1 Bed & Breakfast location

0   10   20   30   40 kilometres
0   10   20   30 miles

Cardigan Bay

Cardigan
Pembrokeshire Coast National Park
Fishguard   Newport
Mathry   Mynydd Preseli
St. David's Head   ▲ 536
St. David's   PEMBROKESHIRE
Ramsey Island
St. Brides Bay   Haverfordwest   A40   Narberth
Milford Haven   Neyland   Pendine
Skomer I.   Pembroke Dock   Saundersfoot
Skokholm I.   Pembroke   Tenby
St. Govan's Head   Carmarthen Bay

Lundy

Hartland Pt.
Hartland

Bude
Poundstock

Boscastle
Tintagel

Port Isaac   Bodmin
Padstow   Wadebridge   Moor
Bodmin   A38   Liskeard
Newquay   CORNWALL
A392   Lostwithiel
St. Austell   Fowey   Looe
St. Agnes   **14**   Polperro
Redruth   Truro   Mevagissey
St. Ives   Camborne Penryn   **15**
Hayle   St. Mawes
St. Just   Marazion   **13**   Falmouth
Penzance   Helston   **12**
11
Land's End
Lizard Pt.   Lizard

St. Martin's
Bryher   Tresco
Hugh Town   St. Mary's

Map 2 23

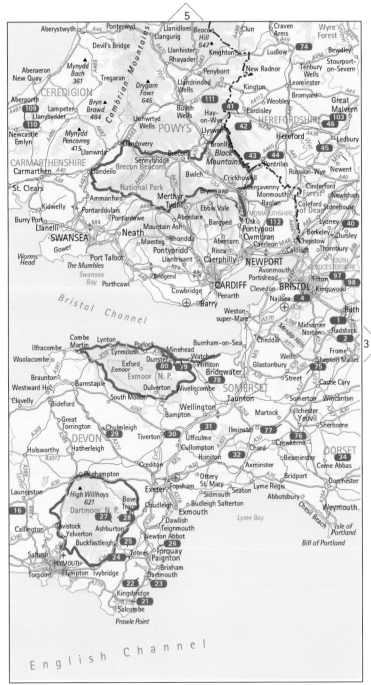

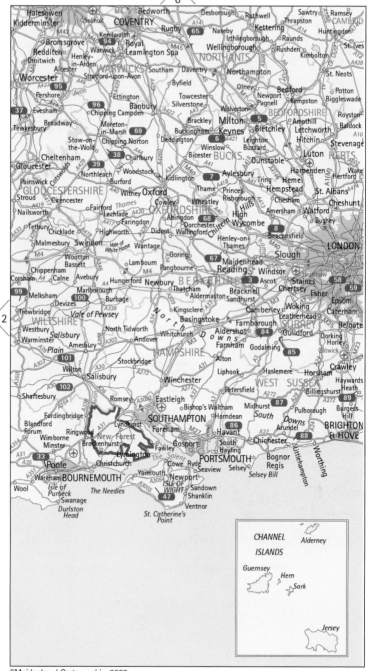

Map 4

25

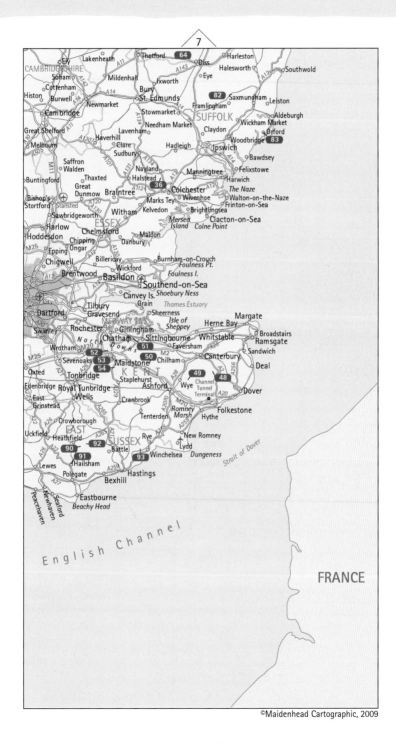

©Maidenhead Cartographic, 2009

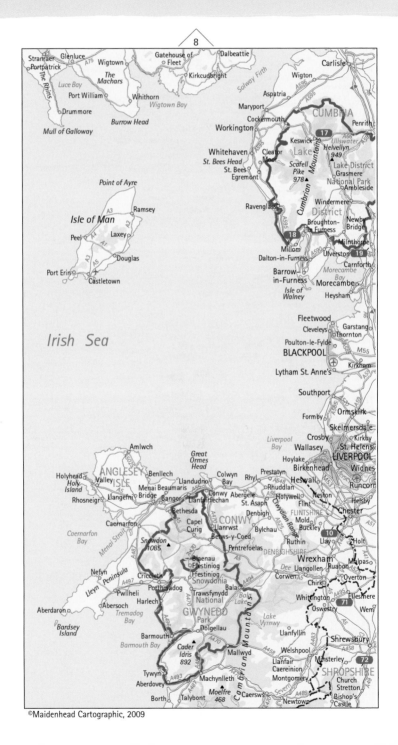

Map 6

27

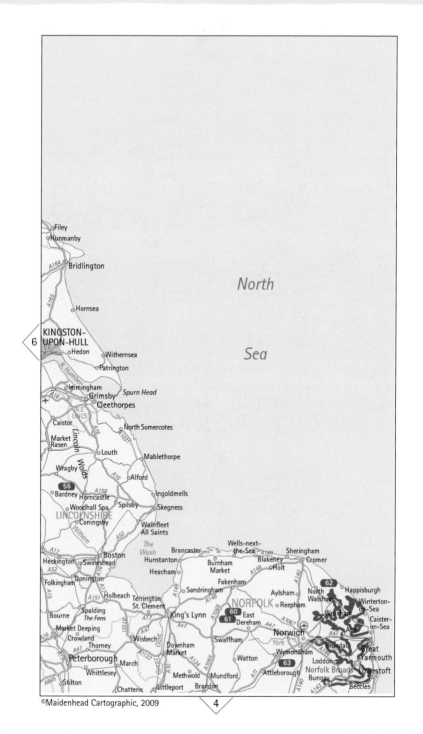

Map 8

29

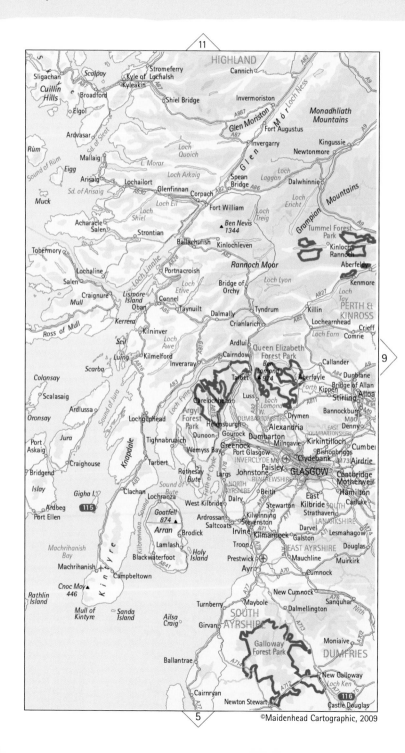

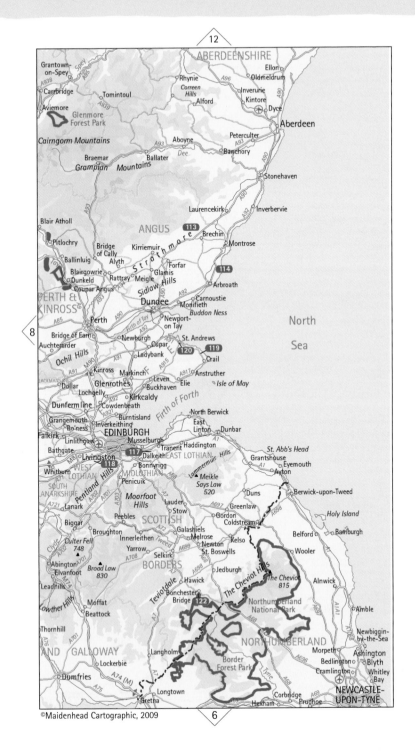

Map 10   31

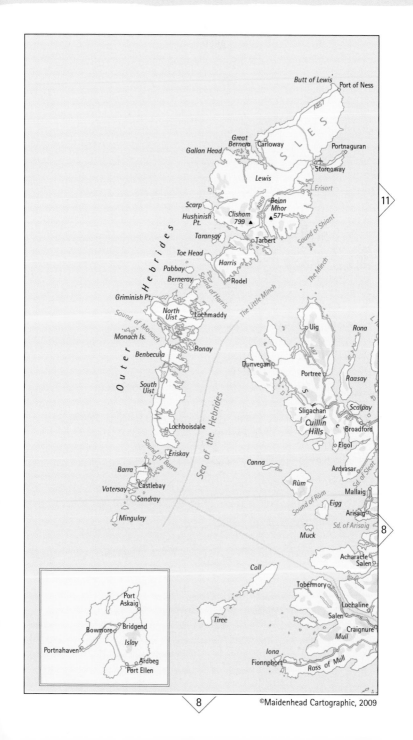

Butt of Lewis
Port of Ness
A857
Great
Bernera Carloway
Gallan Head
I S L E S
Portnaguran
Stornoway
Lewis
Erisort
11
Scarp
A859
Beinn
Mhor
Hushinish   Clisham   571
Pt.   799
Taransay
Tarbert
Sound of Shiant
Toe Head
Harris
Pabbay
Berneray
Rodel
The Minch
Griminish Pt.
Sound of Harris
North
Uist   Lochmaddy
The Little Minch
Sound of Monach
Uig
Rona
Monach Is.
Ronay
A87
Benbecula
Dunvegan
Portree
Raasay
South
Uist
S
Lochboisdale
Sligachan
Scalpay
Cuillin
Hills   Broadford
Elgol
Eriskay
Canna
Ardvasar
Sd. of Sleat
Barra
Sound of Barra
Rùm
Mallaig
Vatersay   Castlebay
Sea of the Hebrides
Sandray
Eigg
Mingulay
Sound of Rùm
Arisaig
Sd. of Arisaig
8
Muck
Acharacle
Salen
Coll
Tobermory
Lochaline
Port
Askaig   Salen
Bowmore   Bridgend   Tiree   Craignure
Islay   Mull
Portnahaven
Ardbeg   Iona
Port Ellen   Fionnphort   Ross of Mull

Outer   Hebrides

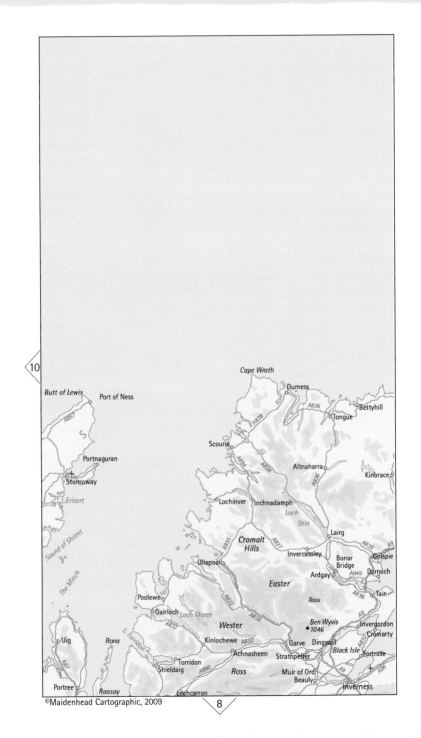

Map 12

33

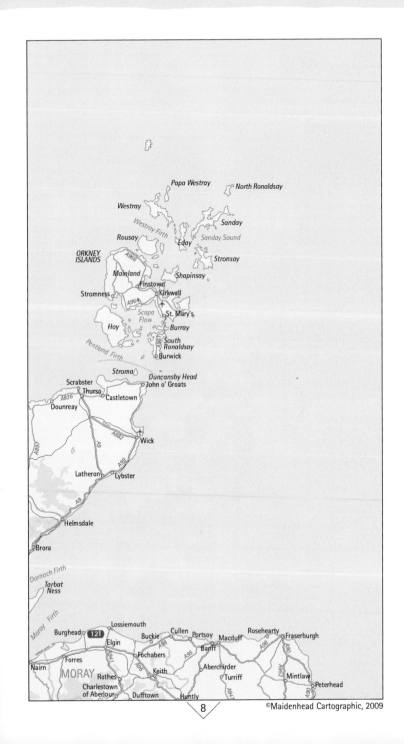

England

Grey Lodge

The garden: A deep love of plants and a collector's delight in finding new treasures have inspired Jane and Anthony's south-west facing terraced garden. The structure was laid out when the house was built in the 1860s, and their most cherished inheritance, a magnificent *Robinia pseudoacacia* was probably planted then. For more than 40 years they have been adding to the garden, planting the series of borders with labour-saving in mind. It's great fun to explore because of its sloping layout and secret paths. The large lawn at the upper level leads to another — and another. A vine planted on the main terrace wall in 1973 now covers 14 metres of wall in three tiers. The soil is free-draining alkaline, in full sun all day, so there is a gravel garden and wildlife pond planted with sun-loving geraniums, alpines, eryngiums, salvias, cistus, euphorbias and species tulips. Drifts of grasses have been blended with herbaceous plants and shrubs for dramatic effect. There is a spring lawn and a vegetable garden. Play boules or soak up the sun and scents on the main lawn, chat to your hosts about special plants, discover botanical treasures. A garden lover's garden with interesting plants to enjoy in every season.

The house: You are in a conservation area, yet just five minutes from the centre of Bath. And the views: breathtaking from wherever you stand. The steep valley rolls out ahead of you from most of the rooms and from the garden comes a confusion and a profusion of scents and colours. The friendly and likeable Sticklands are conservationists too: at breakfast much has been produced locally or from their own garden, jams and marmalades are homemade, teas and coffee Fair Trade. Jane will tell you all about excellent local gardens to visit. *Family room has adjoining room with space for cot. Minimum stay two nights at weekends.*

Price	£80-£90. Singles £50-£55.
Rooms	3: 2 twins/doubles, 1 family room.
Meals	Pub/restaurant 2 miles.
Closed	Rarely.
Directions	From A36, 3 miles out of Bath on Warminster road, take uphill road by lights & viaduct. 1st left, 100 yds, signed Monkton Combe. After village, house 1st on left; 0.5 miles on.

Jane & Anthony Stickland
Grey Lodge, Summer Lane,
Combe Down, Bath BA2 7EU

Tel	01225 832069
Fax	01225 830161
Email	greylodge@surfree.co.uk
Web	www.greylodge.co.uk

Entry 1   Map 2

Hollytree Cottage

The garden: Twenty years of trial and error have gone into creating this cottage garden which slopes gently down from the house to fields below and which complements the house perfectly. It has everything you could want in an open, informal country garden. Very good trees and shrubs including a tamarisk, a white-flowering amelanchier and a soft pink *Magnolia stellata* have been introduced over the years. A tall laburnum flowers profusely in season and Julia's collection of prunus have been carefully planted so that they flower in succession in spring time. A series of irregular beds have been planted with skill and flair. Julia is a keen member of her local horticultural society and buys many treasures at their plant sales, including clematis from the late Betty Risdon who ran the famous Rode Bird Gardens nearby and who was a leading member of the Clematis Society. Fish swim in the little pond, surrounded by water-loving plants, and for fresh vegetables and fruit, there is an immaculate kitchen garden edged with railway sleepers. The small conservatory is packed with the more tender plants, a perfect spot to sit and enjoy the colour and interest outside. The position is delightful and the garden has been designed to make the most of its glorious views. *RHS.*

The house: Meandering lanes lead to this 17th-century cottage – quintessentially English with roses round the door, a grandfather clock in the hall and an air of genteel tranquillity. Julia has updated the cottage charm with Regency mahogany in the inglenook dining room and sumptuous sofas in the sitting room. Bedrooms have long views over farmland and undulating countryside; behind is a conservatory and the sloping, south-facing garden. Ask your hostess about Bath (20 minutes away) – she worked in the Holburne Museum and knows the city well.

Price	£80-£90. Singles £45-£50.
Rooms	3: 1 double, 1 twin, 1 four-poster.
Meals	Pub/restaurant 0.5 miles.
Closed	Rarely.
Directions	From Bath, A36 to Wolverton. Just past Red Lion, turn for Laverton. 1 mile to x-roads; towards Faukland; downhill for 80 yds. On left, just above farm entrance on right.

Mrs Julia Naismith
Hollytree Cottage, Laverton,
Bath BA2 7QZ

Tel	01373 830786
Fax	01373 830786
Email	jnaismith@toucansurf.com
Web	www.hollytreecottagebath.co.uk

Whitehouse Farm Cottage

The garden: Only a quarter of an acre, but Louise and Keir have packed in so much interest with fabulous planting, it seems much larger. This enterprising couple took on an almost blank canvas in 1985 and have now created four 'rooms': the courtyard, the pond garden, the terrace and a circular seating area, all linked by pretty brick paths. To boost the serenity levels there are four water features: a natural pond, a circular 'pot' pond, a D-shaped lily pond and a small water feature with decorative metal fountain. Apart from the mixed traditional hedge round the pond garden (maple, ash, oak, hawthorn and holly) all the trees have been planted by Keir and Louise; a *Magnolia grandiflora* 'Maryland' is their pride and joy. Planting is gorgeously riotous: many climbing roses, honeysuckle, wisteria, solarnum and plenty of herbaceous cottage favourites give colour and scent at the front of the house. At the back, many varieties of fern are happiest near the pond. Herbs also flourish and are used for cooking and tisanes. An army of hedgehogs, toads, frogs, slow worms and bats keeps slugs and snails at bay, while flitting birds happily redistribute seeds. A much-loved garden which you are welcome to wander through – and catch the seasonal surprises.

The house: Garden Cottage – 18th century, timber framed and gorgeous. The Old Forge is equally lovely; both are self-contained farm buildings in which you have complete independence and glorious views. And there's a lovely single room with its own sitting room in the main house where Louise and Keir, film prop makers, live. The house and the cottages are filled with interesting objects and good antiques, beds are comfy and cotton is crisp. Overlooking farmland, this is a surprising find so near to bustling Bracknell – and a fabulous farm shop breakfast sets you up for exploring.

Price	£75–£95. Singles £65–£85.
Rooms	3: 1 single & sitting room. Old Forge: 1 double. Garden Cottage: 1 double & sitting room.
Meals	Picnics by arrangement. Pubsrestaurants within 1 mile
Closed	Christmas & occasionally.
Directions	From A329, B3408 to Binfield. Left at r'bout, left at traffic lights, into St Marks Road. Then 2nd left Foxley Lane, 1st left Murrell Hill Lane. House is 1st on right.

Keir Lusby
Whitehouse Farm Cottage,
Murrell Hill Lane, Binfield RG42 4BY

Tel	01344 423688
Email	garden.cottages@ntlworld.com

21 Royal York Crescent

The garden: Susan's former town garden was regularly open to the public under the National Gardens Scheme; several years ago, armed only with her beautiful sculptures and one or two other things she couldn't bear to leave behind, she embarked on a new venture. Her exotic oasis is now flourishing: brick-edged beds on either side around a central courtyard theme, backed by a high wall with plenty of colourful climbers such as *R.banksiae* 'Lutea' and *Campsis grandiflora.* Large stepping stones set into gravel, with plenty of seating, lend interest, and a wooden, climber-entwined pergola gives height. This is a south-west facing garden and the huge beds contain a mix of architectural plants, some scented shrubs and a quince. The sculptures fit in well with this design-led space; a cube of floating stones with box edging, a ceramic pod surrounded by choysia and a large raised water tank set against a wall of clambering roses; yet another place to sit and breathe in the peaceful serenity. (And who would guess you were a short walk from the city centre?). It is worth coming back from time to time to admire the developments of this peaceful and secluded retreat.

The house: A large, airy and comfortable apartment on the promenade level of this gracious Georgian terrace, reputed to be the longest in Europe – a perfect launch pad for all that the city has to offer. Susan is a relaxed and generous hostess, whose big, terracotta-coloured sitting room with huge views to the Somerset hills is crammed with books, pictures and good furniture; meals are taken at a long table. The guest bedroom, with elegant new bathroom, is down the corridor at the back; wonderfully private, painted in creams and greens with pretty curtains of sprigged arbutus, it has doors to the delightful garden. *Minimum stay two nights at weekends.*

Price	£75.
Rooms	1 double.
Meals	Dinner £20. Restaurants 5-min. walk.
Closed	Occasionally.
Directions	Follow Suspension Bridge signs from city centre to T-junc. opp. Clifton Village's Pizza Provencale. Left down Regent St, then immediately right. House on right, in centre of terrace on upper level.

Mrs Susan Moore
21 Royal York Crescent,
Clifton, Bristol BS8 4JX
Tel   0117 973 4405

Travel Club Offer. See page 290.

South Lodge

The garden: A work in progress. The garden is roughly a long rectangular acre, narrower at the house end, and widening at the bottom to take in an informal pond and the mature trees that were here when Julia arrived. Sixteen years ago the rest was just grass. The first thing to be built was the large pond: 17m by 5m, it is now home to moorhens and visiting ducks, with frogs and newts lurking under the water lilies. At the rear of the house is a formal pond and a seating area, designed by Mark Rendell and surrounded by unusual walls and railings defining different parts of the garden. Guests have their own patio area overlooking a circular lawn and Julia's hot colour border planting; all-year interest is achieved in beds displaying a mixture of perennials and shrubs, old-fashioned roses, hellebores, hostas, day lilies and alstroemerias. Colour themes are pink/purple, yellow/white/blue and warm apricots and oranges. They have also planted about 20 trees for spectacular autumn colour. Favourites are *Liquidambar styraciflua*, *Parrotia persica* and *Quercus palustris*. There are several well-established maples, too, including *Acer griseum*, and a Tibetan cherry tree. Heaps of plans for the future – starting with a vegetable garden.

The house: Handy for the M1, this interestingly developed single-storey building appears pleasant enough. But clever Julia has modern English art, dramatic lighting and contemporary furniture – a look to thrill minimalists. A dark slate corridor lit by fluorescent multicoloured ceiling sticks leads to big, airy bedrooms and hi-spec bathrooms; all generous, all different, with the same crisp modern theme and memory mattresses. Velux blinds are solar-powered, heating is underfoot, rainwater is harvested for loos. You are within walking distance of the Stables Theatre, and Woburn Abbey and Safari Park are close.

Price	£120–£135. Singles £95–£110.
Rooms	3: 2 doubles, 1 family suite.
Meals	Supper, 2 courses, £18.
	Pubs/restaurants within 0.5 miles.
Closed	Occasionally.
Directions	M1 south junc. 13. A421 towards
	Milton Keynes. A5130 towards
	Woburn Sands. After 1 mile left on
	Cross End. House on right.

Julia Cox
South Lodge, 33 Cross End, Wavendon,
Milton Keynes MK17 8AQ

Tel	01908 582946
Email	info@culturevultures.co.uk
Web	www.culturevultures.co.uk

Travel Club Offer. See page 290.

Entry 5   Map 3

The Old Vicarage

The garden: Belinda says it's Hugo who's the gardener: he has the passion and knowledge while she harvests and cooks. The garden's design is part inherited and part created by Hugo over 35 years. It's on several levels, with an unusual shape – the result of bits being added over the years. As well as a rose garden, terraces, a sunken garden, arcades and the charmingly named Phoebe's Garden, there's a romantically overgrown pond presided over by a pair of elegant metal cranes. Hugo plants mainly for leaf-colour combinations: he has more than 50 types of hebe and quite a few rare trilliums and epimediums. The trees (over 40 varieties) provide a protective barrier; some are over a century old. In the big organic kitchen garden, Hugo grows potatoes and asparagus, peas and beans, and – pigeons permitting – brassicas. There's soft fruit, too, and apples, pears, quinces and stone fruit. Any surplus is sold, along with his plants, at the Buckingham Swan Market. The garden is opened for the public on some days each year, but it is also visited by a variety of wildlife, including the occasional barking deer, and a goodly array of birds, from owls and woodpeckers to house martins and finches. *NGS.*

The house: A cracked and bulging wall and rampantly overgrown fence set the tone. This interesting, eccentric Victorian house is not for you if you're fanatically tidy! A porch overflowing with odd shoes, books and gardening clutter leads to a spacious hall with a huge old tapestry and an air of shabby grandeur. The sitting room, dominated by fireplaces at either end, is full of ancestral oils and faded family furniture; the bedrooms are big, old-fashioned and have comfortable beds. Belinda and Hugo are child- and dog-friendly hosts – and you'll get a super welcome from Smaug the chocolate Labrador.

Price	From £60. Singles £35.
Rooms	2: 1 double, 1 twin each with separate bath/shower.
Meals	Pubs within walking distance & 1-2 miles.
Closed	Usually Christmas.
Directions	Padbury is 2 miles south of Buckingham on A413. Head to Thornborough Rd (north of village, west of A413), 1st house on right, behind white fence.

Mrs Belinda Morley-Fletcher
The Old Vicarage,
Padbury MK18 2AH

Tel	01280 813045
Fax	01280 824476
Email	belindamf@freenet.co.uk

 Travel Club Offer. See page 290.

Entry 6   Map 3

The Bunch

The garden: A gorgeous, much-loved, carefully cultivated garden. Bulb-studded borders fringe immaculate lawns and a series of 'rooms' separated by clipped hedging – there are about three acres in all. Mulberry, weeping pear, fruit trees and a sequoia happily share the lawn, while two cypresses flank a formal walk. Guinea fowl parade under frames of 'Rambling Rector' and 'Bobby James'. Pots, urns and statues abound. A Whichford Pottery greyhound on a brick plinth with a curving blue wooden bench calmly gazes down the mown path with its fringe of half standard photinias, to the house. A little Millennium garden with low box hedge manages to be formally informal due to imaginative planting in variously sized beds. Beyond the house is a wild pond shaded by mature trees with a waterfall trickling over old stone. Here, white calling ducks nest. The kitchen and cutting area is a gardeners' delight: soft fruit cages, four compost heaps, vegetable rows, cane tipis for beans and sweet peas, hot and cold greenhouses bursting with seedlings, aviaries and pens. Those of course for the much loved and highly vocal canaries, bantams, guinea hen and golden pheasant. Waddesdon Manor and Claydon House are nearby. *NGS*.

The house: Built in the 18th century for the Duke of Buckingham as staff cottages for the estate, these five have been knocked into one long, low, cosy home. The house is stuffed with a comfortable medley of paintings, old rugs and plenty of squashy-sofa seating. Bedrooms are carpeted (the ground-floor bedroom the more spacious of the two), mattresses are turned after every guest and you are beautifully looked after. Panna and Francis are trustees of charities with an international outreach and have a great interest in people. Listen out for the trilling of the canaries and the clucking of the hens.

Price	£80. Singles £40.
Rooms	2: 1 twin; 1 twin with separate bath.
Meals	Dinner £30. Pub/restaurant 2 miles.
Closed	Easter, Christmas & New Year.
Directions	From Kingswood, A41 for Wotton & Brill. At next 2 T-juncs. left, & left again at sign Wotton only. 1st house on right with staddle stones at gates, which open automatically.

Francis & Panna Newall
The Bunch, Wotton Underwood,
Aylesbury HP18 ORZ

Tel	01844 238376
Fax	01844 237153
Email	newallf@btconnect.com

Travel Club Offer. See page 290.

Entry 7   Map 3

Jean Preston
01296 712640

Guendon Underwood
Shakespeare 01296 770776 HP18 0ST
House

Spindrift

The garden: Norma – "chlorophyll gives me a kick!" – has loved plants since her grandmother took her to Kew when she was very young. As soon as she realised that the garden at Spindrift was a similar shape to Monet's, off she went into arches, walkways, a heavenly series of 'rooms', beautiful herbaceous borders and fountains. It is all on different levels. There's a violet-strewn dell with newts, toads and frogs in the pond, fine lawns to the front flanked by colourful borders and, to one side, a heated, kidney-shaped pool in a sunny raised area with lots of pretty pots (packed with tulips in spring). The fruit and vegetable gardens are terraced down a hill and produce 29 different varieties of vegetable and 13 of fruit, all for the table. There is a large garden room where meals can be served in fine weather, a circular theme for the arched doorways and walkways, and a pristine hosta corner showing off different varieties (not a sign of lace: snails and slugs are somehow deterred) surrounding a raised fountain. Norma is very 'hands on' and often takes children from the school next door around the garden for nature and art. Colours are muted, the softest pinks, blues and mauves backed up by every conceivable green, silver and grey from her beloved hostas.

The house: A long, architect-designed 1933 house in a charming, sleepy village, home of the Quaker Movement; timbers from the *Mayflower* came to rest in an old barn nearby. Much of the house is open to guests and Norma (Constance Spry trained) is an accomplished cook; fruits, herbs and vegetables appear on the table, flowers are beautifully arranged. Traditional bedrooms are super comfortable with excellent beds, powerful new showers, and pretty floral curtains. Swim in the heated pool, walk the stunning countryside, or just slump in the sitting room with its French windows open to the scented garden.

Price	£130. Singles £75.
Rooms	2: 1 double, 1 twin.
Meals	Lunch £25. Dinner, 4 courses, £30. Packed lunch £12.50. Pub 2 miles.
Closed	Never.
Directions	M40 exit 2, take A40 for Gerrards Cross. After 0.5 miles first left into Pot Kiln Lane. Take 2nd left into Jordans, 2nd right by green and past shop. House at end of road on left of school.

Norma Desmond-Mawby
Spindrift,
Jordans HP9 2TE

Tel   01494 873172
Fax   01494 876442
Email   johnmawby@hotmail.com

Ethical Collection: Community; Food. See page 294.

Entry 8   Map 3

The Croft

The garden: A lovely, relaxed garden packed full of cottage favourites and not at all in keeping with the suburban surroundings. Sandra and Rick have lived here for over 20 years and the garden has evolved with them. From the house there is a large south-facing lawn overlooked by a veranda, a vine-covered terrace and a raised terrace surrounded by bamboo and honeysuckle; enjoy an evening drink or a cup of tea here – or choose one of the several benches dotted about the garden. Steps and a slope lead down to the wilder bottom garden with a wildlife pond and reclaimed greenhouse where Rick sows his seeds for blooms the following year; Sandra designs and does the weeding and harvesting – cut flowers for the house and sweet peas every year. It is all highly productive; a small orchard area provides fruit for homemade jams, their own hens pootle about doling out eggs, and the organic vegetable garden yields much for the table. Mature trees – copper beech, conifers and silver birch – are home to plenty of birds; frogs, toads and hedgehogs scuttle underneath. It's all so oasis-like and peaceful you would never imagine Manchester was so close.

The house: What a surprise! Hidden behind trees in serious suburbia is a charming Arts & Crafts house with a smartly painted door; lovely Sandra may greet you with her own delicious scones and plum jam. The entrance hall has a gleaming oak floor and vases of fresh flowers. Most of the Deco features are retained: an extraordinary copper fireplace in the sitting room and wonderful patterned windows. In the bedrooms Shaker meets subtle chintz with stripped floors, tongue and groove furniture and a splash of gingham here and there; bathrooms are ultra modern. A pocket of peace just ten minutes from the airport.

Price	£70. Singles £55.
Rooms	2 doubles.
Meals	Pubs/restaurants within 1 mile.
Closed	Christmas & New Year.
Directions	From Wilmslow centre, south towards Alderley Edge. At Kings Arms roundabout, right towards Knutsford and B5086. Then 1st right on Gravel Lane. After 0.5 miles, entrance gate on bend on left.

Sandra Megginson
The Croft, 103 Gravel Lane,
Wilmslow SK9 6LZ

Tel	01625 523435
Email	thecroftbedandbreakfast@yahoo.co.uk
Web	www.thecroftbedandbreakfastwilmslow.co.uk

Travel Club Offer. See page 290.

The Mount

The garden: Look up – you might catch sight of careering young sparrowhawks testing their wings overhead. Some old and very beautiful trees date back to the building of the house in 1860 while the front garden's acre outline was set out in the early 1950s. Rachel has worked wonders with grounds which were once simply open lawns and trees, developing them gradually over the years, reflecting her, and Jonathan's, growing interest and commitment to gardening. The formality of the new beech-hedged kitchen garden contrasts happily with the more informal mood elsewhere. The front garden's croquet lawn, overlooked by trees, takes you down steps past stone pineapples into the cool seclusion of woodland, with the pink-flushed 'Francis E Lester' rose soaring dizzily up a tall conifer. Roses, clematis and hydrangea sparkle on The Mount's façade as housemartins flit in and out of nests beneath the eaves. Another recent addition is a pond to one side of the house – a mass of bullrushes, foxgloves and iris which is perfect for wildlife. Behind the house the planting is more open and free, decorated with new beech hedges to give shape and form. The handsome pergola is wrapped in wisteria, and a young arbour of willows is settling in nicely. A lovely garden in perfect harmony with the handsome Victorian house. *NGS.*

The house: Peaceful indeed. ("Our guests seem to oversleep", says Rachel.) Britain at its best with a fruitful kitchen garden, scented conservatory, a tennis court, croquet lawn and a genuine welcome. The Victorian house, built for a Chester corn merchant, is furnished in elegant and traditional style, with garden views from every angle. You get a light-filled drawing room, a high-ceilinged dining room, and bedrooms that are most inviting – bright, big, with attractive fabrics, art and lovely furniture. Heaven for garden buffs, walkers, bookworms and birdwatchers (with easy access to Chester and North Wales). *Arrivals from 5pm.*

Price	£70. Singles from £40.
Rooms	3: 2 doubles, 1 twin.
Meals	Pub/restaurant 1-minute walk.
Closed	Christmas & New Year.
Directions	From A55 signed North Wales. Take A5104 Broughton; at 2nd r'bout left to Pennyfordd. Through village, cross over A55 then left Lesters Lane, signed Higher Kinnerton 1.25 miles. House 0.75 miles on right, on the bend.

Jonathan & Rachel Major
The Mount, Higher Kinnerton,
Chester CH4 9BQ

Tel	01244 660275
Email	themount@higherkinnerton.com
Web	www.bandbchester.com

Entry 10   Map 5

Tremayne House

The garden: The Hardmans took on an unstructured two-acre garden and are patiently turning it around. The entrance, through granite piers, leads up a sweeping drive where a shaded border has been created with ferns, tree ferns and shade-tolerant perennials. A circular grass island is cut into a maze pattern, while the formal parterre and box topiary balances the lovely front elevation. The main themes are based on geometric forms of different types; the colour schemes range from whites through to silvers, blues and greys and, further out, mixed colours. The plants themselves may not be rare but they have been put together in an unusual way. The once kitchen garden is the biggest on-going project: now called the Life Garden, it consists of planting around a swimming pool (solar-heated, with whirlpool) and an outdoor eating area complete with fire. Through gates in the wall, Cornish granite steps lead to the long borders and garden 'rooms' walled by beech hedges. The planting is informal herbaceous, again whites, blues and silvers, progressing in autumn to purples, pinks and reds. This is a garden to watch: when the plans are complete the ensemble will be stunning.

The house: Down Cornish lanes, a fine late Regency house and superb B&B. Juliet, easy and vivacious, is a designer with an unusually flamboyant style, so be spoiled by top quality beds, fabulous flowers and candlelit dinners. Bedrooms combine textured chenilles with silks, and checks with chintzes – fabulous; the garden suite is more contemporary but no less plush. This beautifully proportioned house has a sweeping cantilevered staircase, intricate door surrounds, flagstone floors and shuttered windows. You can walk through woods to the Helford river, and the Lizard peninsula is at the door.

Price	From £110. Singles from £90. Suite £120.
Rooms	3: 1 suite & kitchen; 1 double, 1 twin, each with separate bath/shower.
Meals	Dinner £30.
Closed	Christmas & New Year.
Directions	A3083 from Helston. B3293 for St Keverne. After 1.5 miles turn left through Mawgan to St Martin. Just past school left for Mudgeon, on to x-roads. Left & after 200 yds, right. House at end of lane through large granite gate piers.

Anthony & Juliet Hardman
Tremayne House, St Martin-in-Meneage,
Helston TR12 6DA

Tel	01326 231618
Fax	01326 231080
Email	staying@tremaynehouse.com
Web	www.tremaynehouse.com

Glendurgan

The garden: Three Fox brothers created valley gardens near Falmouth in the 1820s: Robert: Penjerrick; Charles: Trebah; Alfred: Glendurgan – which, in 1962, was donated to the National Trust. It's a magical, exotic, heavily shrubbed and wooded place, the tulip trees are some of the largest and oldest in Europe, and there's a sense of fun and discovery as you wend down on steep, superbly maintained paths (pebble-cobbled, bamboo-balustraded) to take a breather on Durgan beach – before climbing back up the other side. It is splendidly scented in spring with camellias, bluebells, primroses and lime-tree flowers. Summer, to quote Charles's excellent book, "breaks in a wave of whiteness, with eucryphia, hoheria, myrtus and that 'bombe Alaska' of rhododendrons, 'Polar Bear', while autumn is awash with bulbs such as amaryllis, colchicum, crinum and nerine." In the winter this is still an important garden in terms of its collection of fine trees, and, even in the wildest weather, a deeply romantic place to be. There is much to explore, including an ancient laurel maze, and Charles will tell you all you want to know; he is a garden designer, trained at Kew and the Inchbald School of Garden Design, and leads garden tours.

The house: In 1827 a thatched cottage stood where the light-filled family house now surveys the valley. Charles's paintings of plants and trees line the large, well-lit stairwell and there are family furniture, books and paintings galore. You eat well: Caroline trained as a cook and her breakfasts draw on the best of local and homemade. Bedrooms have sensational south-facing views; Violet, next to the bathroom, and Magenta, a few yards down the corridor, are as your Edwardian aunt would have liked. No TV but a grand piano, and garden heaven on the doorstep; the view to Helford river through the glen is stunning.

Price	From £85. Singles £70.
Rooms	2 twins sharing bathroom.
Meals	Pubs/restaurants within four miles.
Closed	Occasionally.
Directions	Brown sign to Glendurgan from Mawnan Smith. Ignore signed entrance to garden. Continue on for 200 yards. Take private entrance through white gate on left hand side.

Charles & Caroline Fox
Glendurgan, Mawnan Smith,
Falmouth TR11 5JZ

Tel   01326 250326

Carwinion

The garden: If an inquisitive, errant dinosaur were to come rustling out of the great stands of bamboo or soaring gunnera, you might not be that surprised. These 14 acres are a ravishing homage to leaf, foliage, wildness… a heavenly place of trees, ponds, streams. No wonder that Jane, who has done so much for these grounds in recent years, calls it an "unmanicured garden". At the end of the 19th century, Anthony's grandfather planted the first bamboos in this gorgeous valley garden leading down to the Helford River. Today Carwinion has one of the finest collections in Europe, more than 200 species with wonderful leaf and stem forms… members of the Bamboo Society of Great Britain flock here for annual get-togethers. The lushness soars impressively to the sky – don't miss the 20-foot pieris. Jane has made a series of paths to lead you through one breathtakingly romantic area after another, a palm sheltering under a tall beech tree, a banana tree thriving in the mild atmosphere. Tree ferns soar and, in a final flourish at the foot of the garden, she has transformed an old quarry into an enchanting fern garden. Springtime's azaleas and rhododendrons are a joy. Magic everywhere. *NGS, Good Gardens Guide.*

The house: Come for the setting. This rambling manor began life in 1790 and was enlarged in the 1840s shortly after the garden was designed and planted. Inside: a faded grandeur and a characterful collection of oddities (corkscrews, penknives, magnifying glasses) that successive generations have handed down. Your hosts invite you to share their home with its big old faded bedrooms and bathrooms (not swish). The only sound you'll hear here is the bamboo growing – from that wonderful wild, earthy, primal garden. The walk down to the beach is magical. *Smoking allowed in parts of the house. Minimum stay two nights on bank holiday weekends.*

Price	From £90. Singles £50.
Rooms	3: 1 double, 2 twins/doubles.
Meals	Occasional dinner. Pub 400 yds.
Closed	Rarely.
Directions	Left road in Mawnan Smith at Red Lion pub, onto Carwinion Road. 400 yds up hill on right, sign for Carwinion Garden.

Mr & Mrs A Rogers
Carwinion, Mawnan Smith,
Falmouth TR11 5JA

Tel	01326 250258
Fax	01326 250903
Email	jane@carwinion.co.uk
Web	www.carwinion.co.uk

Entry 13   Map 1

Tregoose

The garden: Alison, who grew up in Cornwall, has an NDH and has created a lovely garden – formal at the front, wilder to the rear and side – that opens to the public thrice yearly. Five fat Irish yews and a tumbledown wall were the starting point… but having reconstructed the walls to create a sunken garden, things started to look up. The L-shaped barn was a good backdrop for planting, so in went cotinus and yellow privet, flame-coloured alstroemerias, show-stopping *Crocosmia solfaterre* (bronze leaves, apricot yellow flowers) and blue agapanthus for contrast. The sunken walled garden protects such tender treasures as *Aloysia citrodora*, leptospermum, and, pièce de résistance, *Acacia baileyana purpurea*. Palm-like dracaena, Monterey pines and cypresses and the Chusan palm do well, and you can't miss the spectacular magenta blooms of the 30-foot *Rhododendron arboreum* 'Cornish Red'. The woodland garden displays more muted colours, scented deciduous azaleas, and the white July-scented rhododendron 'Polar Bear'. Over 60 varieties of snowdrop flower from November to March – spectacular. The potager supplies produce for dinners and flowers for the house, and Alison can supply almost any information about Cornish plants and gardens. *NGS, Cornwall Garden Society.*

The house: Tregoose is a handsome, late-Regency country house surrounded by rolling countryside. In the drawing room, where a log fire is lit on cooler evenings, a rare and beautiful Chinese cabinet occupies one wall and in the dining room is a Malayan inscribed silk screen – a thank you present from Empire days. Upstairs, lovely, comfortable, period bedrooms have antique furniture, views onto the glorious garden and pretty bathrooms with generous baths. At the head of the Roseland Peninsula yet conveniently near the A390 this is a great ensemble: house, garden, hosts and charming pets. *Children by arrangement.*

Price	From £98.
Rooms	3: 1 twin, 1 four-poster; 1 double with separate bath.
Meals	Dinner from £28. BYO. Pub/restaurant 1 mile.
Closed	Christmas & Easter.
Directions	A30 for Truro, at Fraddon bypass left for Grampound Rd. After 5 miles, right onto A390 for Truro; 100 yds, right where double white lines end. Between reflector posts to house, 200 yds down lane.

Alison O'Connor
Tregoose, Grampound,
Truro TR2 4DB

Tel	01726 882460
Fax	01872 222427
Web	www.tregoose.co.uk

The Wagon House

The garden: As the Wagon House lies in the centre of Heligan Gardens (just over the wall from the Sundial Garden), Charles and Mally Francis would be the first to admit that most people are here to visit their neighbour's garden rather than their own! However, their small garden will undoubtedly give encouragement to those who are just starting out with a long-neglected patch. They have eradicated the brambles and nettles, and unearthed a Mini car door from the flower bed in the process – together with some nice slate slabs. Now they are developing a garden which includes the plants that thrive in the Cornish coastal climate: hydrangeas, cordylines, griselinias and phormiums, a New Zealand tree fern, ceanothus, small palms, a crinodendron and a grevillea. In spite of Heligan's popularity, the Wagon House sits in a private spot undisturbed by visitors – while a short walk (of about 400 yards) up the tree-lined drive brings you to the Gardens. Charles is a garden photographer and Mally is a botanical artist, so both are closely involved with Heligan and can provide rare insights. As they are professionally involved with the Eden Project, too, they have been part of its development from the earliest days and so are exceptional hosts.

The house: The 18th-century wagoners would be amazed if they could see it all today. Spotless bedrooms in what used to be the joiner's workshop upstairs, and, where the wagons rolled in, five huge windows through which the morning light streams, along with the dawn chorus. There's tea in the cheerful sitting room or in the summerhouse on arrival; breakfast consists of Aga-cooked local farm produce – to keep up the energy levels for Heligan, the Eden Project and innumerable Cornish gardens. Across the drive, courses in botanical art are held in the Saw-Pit Studio with your cheery, friendly hosts. *Minimum stay two nights.*

Price	£90. Singles £50.
Rooms	2 twins sharing separate bath (let to same party only).
Meals	Pub/restaurant 2 miles.
Closed	Christmas & New Year.
Directions	From St Austell for Heligan Gardens. Follow private drive towards Heligan House. Left before white gateposts, keep left past cottages, left after The Magnolias and follow drive.

Charles & Mally Francis
The Wagon House, Heligan Manor,
St Ewe, St Austell PL26 6EW

Tel	01726 844505
Email	thewagonhouse@mac.com
Web	www.thewagonhouse.com

Hornacott

The garden: A dynamic garden where lots has been happening in recent years as Jos and Mary-Anne work their way from one area to the next. The garden is about one-and-a-half acres of sloping ground with shady spots, open sunny lawns and borders and many shrubs. A stream tumbles through the garden after heavy rain and trickles quietly by in the dryer summer months; its banks are being cleared and water-loving plants introduced. Elsewhere, clearance is underway, too, and by opening up long-hidden areas, wildflowers have been given space and light to thrive. A charming pergola with its own seat has been built at one end of the garden to add vertical interest and a touch of formality. The recent loss of some mature trees near the house has been a blessing in disguise – creating open spaces where there was once too much shade. Your hosts have been busy planting rhododendrons, azaleas, camellias and many flowering shrubs and everything is being designed to blend with the peaceful setting and the backdrop of grand old trees. A collection of David Austin roses has been introduced – his are the only ones which seem to do well here, says Mary-Anne. There's plenty of colour too, with varied colour themings from one border to the next.

The house: The garden has seats poised to catch the evening sun: perfect after a day exploring the gardens and beaches of Cornwall. The peaceful house is named after the hill and you have a private entrance to your fresh, roomy suite: a twin-bedded room and a large, square, high sitting room with double doors, which looks onto the wooded valley. There are chocolates and magazines and a CD player, and you are utterly private; Jos, a kitchen designer, and Mary-Anne really want you to enjoy your stay. Local produce is yours for delicious breakfast and dinner.

Price	From £80. Singles £50.
Rooms	1 suite; 1 single with separate shower.
Meals	Dinner, 3 courses, £20. BYO.
Closed	Christmas.
Directions	B3254 Launceston-Liskeard. Through South Petherwin, down steep hill, last left before little bridge. 1st on left.

Jos & Mary-Anne Otway-Ruthven
Hornacott, South Petherwin,
Launceston PL15 7LH

Tel	01566 782461
Fax	01566 782461
Email	stay@hornacott.co.uk
Web	www.hornacott.co.uk

 Travel Club Offer. See page 290.

Entry 16   Map 2

Spooney Green

The garden: Sandra and Ian's greatest love is the natural world. In nine years they have created a magical garden out of what was just boggy fields; now the basic plan is to create more formal gardens around the house, moving down through bog area, the pond and then on into a wildflower meadow. Another area has been set aside for a productive fruit and vegetable garden, and for Sandra's beehives. Secluded spaces have been created to sit and enjoy the bird and animal life that now abounds. Terraces at the front of the house face south and are a peaceful place to enjoy the stunning views of the western Lake District fells. Flower beds are crammed with cottage garden favourites, which attract bees and other pollinating insects. An ancient lime tree is in full flower in July and the lime honey produced will find its way to your breakfast table. This committed couple garden organically and enjoy eating what they produce: soft fruits for jams and for breakfast in season, eggs from their hens, honey from the hives. If they are not out walking or birdwatching you will find them in the garden; not a day goes by without one of them having a 'good idea' – and they sell surplus plants.

The house: Views down the long garden, across the invisible road and to the hills are heart-lifting. The traffic hum is quickly forgotten in the comfortable house with a strong pine theme. There is no sitting room and you breakfast at two separate tables, but on a sunny day you may sit in the garden for hours, and soak up the enthusiasms of Sandra and Ian. You sleep in simple, comfortable and unpretentious bedrooms – a massive relief to the walkers who lope down the great Skiddaw hill right behind. Stoke up on homemade muesli, home-baked bread from locally milled flour, and Ian's homemade potato cakes – delicious.

Price	£70. Singles £60.
Rooms	3: 2 doubles; 1 double with separate shower.
Meals	Packed lunch £5. Pub/restaurant 500 yds.
Closed	Rarely.
Directions	From Keswick take Carlisle road. Right after hospital, continue for 300 yds then left up unmetalled lane. House is at the top.

Sandra Wallace
Spooney Green, Spooney Green Lane,
Keswick CA12 4PJ
Tel   01768 772601
Email   spooneygreen@tiscali.co.uk

Entry 17   Map 5

Broadgate

The garden: The terrible storms two years ago felled several trees in the garden but improved the views to the woods and sea enormously; the setting is glorious. This is a classic Cumbrian country house garden, 300 years old, complete with stone balustrade and planters, box garden and fragrant roses, venerable trees and lashings of rhododendron and azalea. With the spring come wave upon wave of snowdrops (2,500 were planted last spring) and merry daffodils. A walled garden, engagingly faded in its woodland setting, tells of gardeners and summers long ago. High stone walls, covered with climbers and old roses, enclose wide herbaceous beds and an old glasshouse. At the front of the house, vivid 'Greek' blue hydrangeas make a startling contrast to the dazzling white façade and smooth green lawns, while an old palm tree adds an exotic touch. This is a garden which still needs much work to restore it but Diana has plans. Its bones are good, the position is wonderful and the potential enormous. There's masses of birdlife, too, including flycatchers and green woodpeckers. Down the lane are some interesting old buildings belonging to the estate farm, where chickens peck around under the trees and cattle graze.

The house: Passing white stone gate pillars, the drive sweeps up to the Georgian symmetry of a big white house – big but not intimidating. The Lewthwaites have been here for ever and the grand rooms have a lovely, lived-in feel. Guests have the whole of the third floor to themselves: gorgeous flowery bedrooms with high, comfortable beds and pretty mahogany furniture. There's a little sitting room and a breakfast room with floor-to-ceiling, china-filled cupboards. Diana, an ex-Olympic skier, is an accomplished cook. Walk it off in the garden with its stunning views to the estuary. *Children over ten welcome.*

Price	£80. Singles £45.
Rooms	4: 2 doubles sharing bath (let to same party only); 2 singles sharing shower (same party only).
Meals	Supper, 3 courses, £18.50. Pub 5.2 miles.
Closed	Rarely.
Directions	M6 junc. 36. After 3 miles, left slip road A590 to Barrow. After 17 miles, right A595, Workington and Millom. After 11 miles, traffic lights and bridge; 3 miles right to Broadgate.

Diana Lewthwaite
Broadgate, Millom,
Broughton-in-Furness LA18 5JY
Tel   01229 716295
Email   dilewthwaite@bghouse.co.uk

Barn Close

The garden: A lovely, two-acre garden with something to interest the garden lover at any time of the year. Fantastic displays of snowdrops, aconites and bluebells in spring, a swathe of autumn colour from the surrounding mature trees, and a large herbaceous border that's stunning in June and July. Mike organises birdwatching breaks around the local area but you need not go very far: over the last ten years nearly 80 different species have been seen from or in the garden. Anne has planted teasels, acanthus, grasses and anything with seedheads to attract the birds but, needless to say, they are equally keen on her productive vegetable garden and fruit trees. The pond has been supplemented with water irises, candelabra primulas and water lilies: wildlife flourishes, particularly dragonflies, and a good number of resident butterflies. This is a beautiful unspoiled part of Cumbria (AONB), with lovely views and good walks round Morecambe Bay, famous for its huge flocks of wading birds. There are many places of interest nearby including Levens Hall, Sizergh Castle (NT) and Holker Hall, while the Lakeland Horticultural Society garden is a gem overlooking Lake Windermere. The plant centre in the village, Beetham Nurseries, won a much coveted gold medal at the Tatton RHS show 2008. *RHS, HPS, Lakeland Horticultural Society, Cumbria Gardens Trust.*

The house: A 1920s house in the village with lots of windows, high chimneys and well-proportioned rooms off long and spacious corridors. Bedrooms — one with long views over the garden — are traditional, comfortable and lack pretension; bathrooms (not huge) are spanking clean. Supper is by arrangement but will include home-grown vegetables and is taken in the dining room at a solid mahogany table. Anne is able to give her visitors lots of personal attention and this is certainly good value — perfect for bird lovers, walkers and anyone seeking a bit of peace and quiet away from the crowds.

Price	£44-£60. Singles £28-£35.
Rooms	3: 1 twin; 1 twin, 1 single with separate bath/shower.
Meals	Supper £18. Tray snack £7-£10. Pub 300 yds.
Closed	Christmas.
Directions	Exit M6 junc. 35 for 4 miles. A6 north to Milnthorpe & Beetham. Left before bridge; right at Wheatsheaf pub & church. Right after wall at end of village. Over cattle grid. At end of drive.

Anne Robinson
Barn Close,
Beetham LA7 7AL

Tel	01539 563191
Fax	01539 563191
Email	anne@nwbirds.co.uk
Web	www.nwbirds.co.uk/bcindex.htm

Entry 19   Map 5

Cascades Gardens

The garden: A superb four-acre garden on multi levels. Alan provides the ideas for the landscaping and the muscle to develop it, Elizabeth takes care of the planting – brilliantly! Over 4,000 specimens and more than 100 different perennials clamour for attention in herbaceous borders backed by large shrubs, then high banks and mature trees; copper beech, ancient yews and dozens of newcomers, planted for bark interest, blossom and autumn colour. The ruins of an old mill and a lead mine are now integral; a babbling brook, ponds and small waterfalls somersault right through... expect an abundance of water plants, marginals and a whole host of perennials. A wildflower bank sits happily with more cultivated areas; variegated laurels and cascading plants cheer a bleak winter; hellebores and bulbs strain for spring. In summer the different parts of the garden are lush and sheltered with plenty of places to sit and admire in peace and quiet. Plants here are mostly grown from root cuttings or seed and many of them are unusual; their *Enkianthus campanulatus* was borrowed for an exhibition at the Chelsea Flower Show. In the evening, amble down to the pond and see moorhens and mallards, flitting bats and frogs galore. Many cuttings are for sale.

The house: The late-Georgian mill manager's house has a stunning setting: a shrub-strewn cliff rising behind, gorgeous gardens with waterfalls below. Alan and Elizabeth do warm, traditional B&B; breakfasts include tasty Derbyshire oat cakes, bathrooms flaunt fluffy towels. Indian and Tibetan art is a passion and the house is filled with pictures and artifacts from the orient. No sitting room but bedrooms are super-comfortable; the new suite sports leather armchairs, spa bath and a waterfall view. Breakfast is served in the cosy dining room, its window filled with luscious plants. Great houses and Arkwright's Mill await your discovery.

Price	£80–£88. Suite £104.
Rooms	3: 2 doubles.
	Garden annexe: 1 suite for 2.
Meals	Pub 0.5 miles.
Closed	Christmas & New Year.
Directions	A6 Derby to Cromford, then Via Gellia to Bonsall. 1 mile right into village. 800 yds on right before village green.

Alan & Elizabeth Clements
Cascades Gardens, Clatterway Hill,
Bonsall, Matlock DE4 2AH

Tel	01629 822464
Fax	0115 947 0014
Email	enquiries@cascadesgardens.com
Web	www.cascadesgardens.com

Higher Beeson House

The garden: There's lots going on here. What started as four acres of boggy wilderness which Lynda and Charles hoped would 'gradually evolve' has become a super garden that is clearly loved. It started with the pond, now stocked with rudd, visited by mallards and moorhens, and packed with flag irises and lilies. Then a series of steps and terraces (all built by clever Charles), bubbling fountains, timber decks, a waterfall, and a greenhouse. Lynda is the plantswoman and she goes for big plants! Gunnera, bamboo, echiums and a banana plant all zoom heavenward while yuccas, phormiums and agapanthus add to the exotic feel. In the perennial bed there are more traditional plants like roses and stocks. The gentle climate allows bougainvillea and hibiscus to grow alongside a vine and a fig, and even olives in a sheltered spot. Vegetables, soft fruit and herbs grow happily, and the greenhouse produces chillies and sweet peppers in abundance. There are willows and alders around the pond and spruce, firs, oaks, ash, chestnut and rowan in the woodland area. So peaceful, so much wildlife; pick a bench and delight in it all. Sometimes you can hear the sea.

The house: The farmhouse and stables, arranged around a neat yard, started life in the 16th century, but are now kitted out with ground-source underfloor heating and solid oak floors. Lynda and Charles give you a great local breakfast in the beamed dining room with views through the kitchen to the garden. Bedrooms are in the stables: enter through a green tiled hall where there is a drying room and a communal fridge for fresh milk or a bottle of wine. All are a good size, newly carpeted, spotlessly clean and with good lighting. You have a deeply chic summer house by the lake, with a wood-burning stove and comfy chairs.

Price	£76–£90.
Rooms	3: 1 double, 1 four-poster, 1 family room.
Meals	Dinner, 3 courses, £22. Pub/restaurant 0.75 miles.
Closed	Rarely.
Directions	From Kingsbridge, A379 to Stokenham. Right at mini roundabout, follow road for about a mile then left into Beeson. Right at sign to Beeson Farm. House is 200 yds from junction on left.

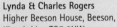

Lynda & Charles Rogers
Higher Beeson House, Beeson,
Kingsbridge TQ7 2HW

Tel 01548 580623
Fax 01548 580623
Email enquiry@higher-beeson.co.uk
Web www.higher-beeson.co.uk

Greenswood Farm

The garden: Roger has a huge interest in countryside management, having worked on The Coast Path and restoring Green Lanes in the South Hams. Helen adores growing flamboyant flowers (and arranges them skilfully in the house). When they moved here eleven years ago they inherited a large garden planted on a boggy field with a stream running through and some mature shrubs and trees. Enlarged and landscaped, it has been designed to reflect the contours of its hilly, wooded outer borders. Perfect beds and borders are packed with spring bulbs, primroses, rhododendrons and azaleas, and pathways and older beds have been discovered and restored. Water lovers such as the gigantic *Gunnera manicata*, white irises, ferns and grasses hug the ponds while there are delightful secret pathways through colourful borders with large shrubs; new paths take you across the fields and through the woods to another pond, or through a bluebell wood, over the fields and back to the house. Terracing some of the steeper areas has created quiet places to sit and take in the views. The orchard is being restored, the planting around the ponds developed; the final pond is on level ground, hidden from the house with views of Greenswood Valley. Birdsong, ancient woodland, glorious peace.

The house: A lovely Devon longhouse covered in wisteria, with stone flagging, deep window sills, elegant furniture. But this is a working farm and there is no stuffiness in Helen and Roger – you will find a warm and cosy place to relax and enjoy the gorgeous valley that is now their patch. You have a separate staircase to sunny, south-facing bedrooms with garden views, huge mirrors, colourwashed walls, old pine and pretty fabrics. Organic beef and lamb are reared on the farm and breakfast eggs come straight from Sally Henny Penny outside; buy some to take home – if you can drag yourself away. *Minimum stay two nights in summer.*

Price	From £75. Singles from £60.
Rooms	3: 2 doubles, 1 twin.
Meals	Dinner (min. 4) by arrangement. Pubs/restaurants 1.5 miles.
Closed	Rarely.
Directions	A381 for Dartmouth. At Golf & Country Club right to Strete. Signpost after 1 mile.

Mrs Helen Baron
Greenswood Farm, Greenswood Lane,
Dartmouth TQ6 OLY

Tel	01803 712100
Email	stay@greenswood.co.uk
Web	www.greenswood.co.uk

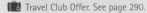 Travel Club Offer. See page 290.

Knocklayd

The garden: The starting point is an exceptional site, high above the village of Kingswear and its more bumptious neighbour Dartmouth, across the water; gardening here is a delight with the steep views of the town, estuary and harbour dramatically lovely, while hoots from the steam train trundling below give a wonderfully nostalgic feel. The smallish, multi-levelled plot is approached via a lavender and thyme border that takes you up to the house; the rest of the garden wraps itself comfortably around two sides and Susan has kept things simple, scented and colourful, never brash. She has now completed three terraces, including the circular pad from which you are at eye level with the Naval College; the next area takes you past a fabulous eucalyptus and the third is the lowest, very sheltered, lawn. The different areas are demarcated with gently shaped beds and grouped planting: spirea, agapanthus, choisya, nothing too formal or jarring on the eye. Guests are encouraged to choose a sheltered spot in which to sit and contemplate. This is a lovely, relatively low-maintenance garden with some gravel and paved areas, groundcover and shrubs (euphorbia, cistus, hebe) along with some old family favourites like cyclamen, camellia and Lady's Mantle.

The house: Built in 1905, this family house makes the most of extraordinary views of estuary and harbour; the sitting rooms and pretty bedrooms each take a different angle. Susan, who imports lovely things from India, has beautifully coordinated soft-coloured fabrics, carpets and wallpapers, and added family furniture, prints, paintings and general 'abilia'. They've lived all over – he was a naval attaché – and welcome dogs, too; Molly the bichon will make friends with yours. Boating can be arranged, trains met, nothing is too much trouble. And breakfast? Locally smoked haddock, salmon and scrambled eggs, homemade jams and smoothies.

Price	£100. Singles £60.
Rooms	3: 2 doubles, 1 twin/double.
Meals	Supper & dinner from £25. Pub/restaurant 400 yds.
Closed	Rarely.
Directions	To Kingswear on B3205, left fork for Kingswear and Lower Ferry. Down hill, 1 mile, road climbs and becomes one-way. Fork left into Higher Contour Road, half mile on left into Redoubt Hill; park below red gate; signed.

Susan & Jonathan Cardale
Knocklayd, Redoubt Hill,
Kingswear TQ6 0DA

Tel	01803 752873
Email	stay@knocklayd.com
Web	www.knocklayd.com

7 The Grove

The garden: John and Bethan set out to create a peaceful and sheltered space in the middle of a busy and lively town – but they have done more than that. Here is an enchanting garden of surprises which all are welcome to roam. It's about a quarter of an acre in size and begins with a small courtyard area filled with pots, then up more steps to three small ponds, fed by rainwater from the house, and supplying the garden with frogs and newts. Beyond these are riotous flower beds separated by grass in which wildflowers are allowed to romp – dandelions, primroses, daisies. John is tolerant with the slugs and encourages the self-seeded to survive. Poppies, rocket, honesty, hollyhocks, forget-me-nots and columbine rub shoulders with more formal planting; fruit and fir trees provide shade and roses, honeysuckle, clematis and blackberries scramble up walls. In summer the greenhouse groans with tomatoes and grapes, along with hibiscus, oleander and a bright red geranium. Behind a large stone wall there is a vegetable and fruit garden where priority is given to produce that is good to pick at and eat raw. Bethan and John love the garden but don't try to control it too much; they are more interested in creating shapes and spaces, appreciating light, shade and the seasons, and watching wildlife. Bliss.

The house: In the heart of lovely, higgledy-piggledy Totnes, find a whitewashed house with pert blue windows and doors, friendly Bethan and John, homemade biscuits, pretty flowers and good art. Guests have an open-plan room, painted white, for delicious breakfasts of homemade bread and jam, local bacon and eggs, soft fruit from the garden. Bedrooms are light, bright and uncluttered (one with its own little sitting room), with wooden floors, excellent beds and handsome rugs; bathrooms bulge with big fluffy towels. You are a stone's throw from super places to eat, and you can walk to Dartington along the river.

Price	£80. Singles £50.
Rooms	2 twins/doubles sharing bath (let to same party only).
Meals	Pubs/restaurants 300 yds.
Closed	Christmas.
Directions	From A38 turn to Buckfastleigh and Totnes. In Totnes, straight on at 1st set lights. By garage take right lane, then exit for town centre. Next r'bout straight across, follow St Katherines Way. After 200 yds right into Victoria St then into The Grove. House on right.

Bethan Edwards & John Paige
7 The Grove,
Totnes TQ9 5ED

Tel	01803 862866
Email	totnesgrove@yahoo.com
Web	www.totnesgrove.com

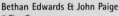

Kingston House

The garden: The whole place is an absolute gem for purists and nature lovers alike. Elizabeth's love of wildlife has made restoring the garden no easy task – she is adamant that no pesticides be used – but most of the estate was in need of a complete overhaul when she arrived. Now it is perfectly renovated and opens for the National Gardens Scheme three times a year: a rosy walled garden with peaches, pears, greengages and nectarines intertwined with roses and jasmine, beech hedging with yew arches, a formal rose garden, box topiary, a dear little summer house edged with lavender, an orchard with rare apples, and, in the South Garden, an avenue of pleached limes leading to a wild woodland. Elizabeth is also a stickler for historical accuracy. New projects include a fountain and mulberry garden and a huge patterned box parterre for either side of the front drive (4,000 plants were propagated on site) interplanted with conical yews and parrot tulips for the spring – the height of fashion when the house was built! The vegetable garden is productive and neat with a nod to the contemporary – unusually shaped twigs and branches are used as natural sculptures for supporting beans and sweet peas. *NGS.*

The house: Gracious and grand is this impeccably-restored former home of a wealthy wool merchant with all its trappings intact. A rare marquetry staircase, an 18th-century painted china closet, marble works, original baths, galleried landings and oak panelling to gasp at. But it's not austere – the bedrooms are steeped in comfort and cushions, a fire roars in the guest sitting room (formerly the chapel), food is fresh, delicious and home-grown, and breakfasts outstanding. Rugged Dartmoor is to the north, Totnes minutes away and walks from the house through the gentle South Hams are spectacular.

Price	From £180. Singles from £110.
Rooms	3: 2 doubles; 1 double with separate bath.
Meals	Dinner £38. Pubs/restaurants 2-5 miles.
Closed	Christmas & New Year.
Directions	From A38, A384 to Staverton. At Sea Trout Inn, left fork for Kingston; halfway up hill right fork; at top, ahead at x-roads. Road goes up, then down to house; right to front of house.

Travel Club Offer. See page 290.

Michael & Elizabeth Corfield
Kingston House,
Staverton, Totnes TQ9 6AR

Tel	01803 762235
Fax	01803 762444
Email	info@kingston-estate.co.uk
Web	www.kingston-estate.co.uk

Entry 25   Map 2

Cary Court

The garden: Across the front of the south-facing house is a lovely veranda, home to a most prolific datura with huge, cream-coloured, trumpet-shaped flowers; the scent in the summer evenings is almost overwhelming. Two others in a border sport orange flowers, just as highly scented. Japanese bananas flower and fruit in abundance – not edible but thrilling – and in amongst these are clumps of birds of paradise with their beak-like flowers appearing in spring. There are large orange and lemon bushes and many species of palm trees including two massive Chusan palms, cordylines, bamboo, and both red and white parrot's bill. Moving down through the garden there is a fence which in summer is covered in jasmine and chocolate vine. In a corner by the water feature there are clumps of arum and ginger lilies, and something very exciting which grew from a dormant tuber: *Cardiocrinum giganteum* – a giant lily that can grow to ten feet! One half expects to see a chap in a pith helmet peering out through this lot, and the treats go on: yuccas, castor oil trees, massive tree ferns, a fig tree and flowering fatsia, gunnera, agapanthus and – right at the bottom – a koi carp pond surrounded by hostas and euphorbia, more palms and bananas. Wow.

The house: Disraeli lived next door and Lily Langtry had a house around the corner in the days when this was a popular seaside resort – and you can still get the train here; Paul will pick you up from the station. Once up the steep drive you are immersed in a proper 'plantation style' house, but a short walk away from the bustle. Find no surprises in the décor – a mix of antique and reproduction furniture, brocade pale-gold sofas, oriental side lamps, and uncluttered bedrooms. It is all squeaky clean and comfortable and there's an exercise room, a heated pool, huge breakfasts; your hosts are charming and affable.

Price	£65–£90. Singles £45–£55.
Rooms	11: 7 doubles, 2 twins, 2 four-posters.
Meals	Pubs/restaurants 0.25 miles.
Closed	Christmas & New Year.
Directions	From harbour left at clock tower roundabout onto Babbacombe Road. Pass museum, then left into Braddon Hill Road East. At hill top right into Hunsdon Road. Second drive on left.

Linda & Paul Garwood
Cary Court,
Hunsdon Road, Torquay TQ1 1QB

Tel	01803 209205
Fax	01803 201003
Email	stay@carycourthotel.co.uk
Web	www.carycourthotel.co.uk

Travel Club Offer. See page 290.

Corndonford Farm

The garden: Climb and climb the Dartmoor edge with views growing wider and wilder all the time until you reach the stone-walled lane and the sturdy granite buildings of Corndonford Farm. Roses and wisteria clamber up the rugged façade, softening the ancient strength of the house. At jam-making time the air is filled with the sweetness of an enormous pan of bubbling strawberries. Ann's jewel-like little farm garden has an arched walk of richly scented honeysuckle, roses and other climbers which leads to her very productive vegetable and soft fruit garden – the source of the berries. She knows her plants and has created a small, cottagey garden in complete harmony with its surroundings. There's a rockery and a little gravelled patio just outside the house which has been planted with charming cottage flowers. Above is a lawn edged by deep borders absolutely packed with colour and traditional cottage garden plants, including salmon-pink rhododendron, cranesbill and lupins. Do take the short walk along the lane to Ann's second garden, known locally as the "traffic calmer". Here, by the roadside, she has planted loads of rhododendrons and shrubs in a delightful display – and it really does encourage even the most hurried motorists to slow down. The views are breathtaking, the setting wonderfully peaceful, the garden as informal and welcoming as Ann and Will themselves.

The house: Come to be engrossed in the routines of a wild, engagingly chaotic haven. Ann and Will are friendly, kind and extrovert; guests adore them and keep coming back. There is comfort, too: warm curtains, a four-poster with lacy drapes, early morning tea. Gentle giant shire horses live at the shippon end where the cows once stood, and there's medieval magic with Bronze Age foundations. A wonderful place for those who love the rhythm and hubbub of real country life – and the Two Moors Way footpath is on the doorstep. *Children over ten by arrangement.*

Price	£60–£70. Singles £35.
Rooms	2: 1 twin, 1 four-poster sharing bath.
Meals	Pub 2 miles.
Closed	Rarely.
Directions	From A38 2nd Ashburton turn for Dartmeet & Princetown. In Poundsgate pass pub on left; 3rd right on bad bend signed Corndon. Straight over x-roads, 0.5 miles, farm on left.

Ann & Will Williams
Corndonford Farm, Poundsgate,
Newton Abbot TQ13 7PP

Tel   01364 631595
Email   corndonford@btinternet.com

Ethical Collection: Food.
See page 294 for details

Entry 27   Map 2

The Old Rectory

The garden: Rachel has been "dotty about gardening" since she was a child and here she has used her artistic talent to create an organic cottage garden with a twist. Wanting the garden to reflect the symmetry of the house and then merge into the Dartmoor landscape, she has developed it from what was merely a field and a sloping lawn. Herbaceous borders hug the sides and are crammed with old favourites and many wildflowers. Half-way down is a sunny terrace for lounging, a border of scented roses and a heather bank reflecting the Moor. Then down through two labyrinth paths mown into the grass to a little stone circle and an open meadow that borders the woodland garden. The walled garden bursts with soft fruit and apple trees and a willow tunnel takes you to an old pond and bog garden fed by a stream and surrounded with primula, iris and other bog plants. This year has seen the new South African garden – a riot of agapanthus, crocosmia, dierama and more. Lovely arty touches everywhere – peep-holes through hedges, secret places, benches cut into the bottoms of old trees, willow structures and plenty of room for Rachel and Heather's sculptures. Rachel was told she couldn't grow roses on Dartmoor but her successes are everywhere, from the ramblers she loves to the old Georgian era varieties that go so well with the house.

The house: The former home of the vicar of Widecombe with its famous fair and "Uncle Tom Cobbley and all" oozes tranquillity and calm. One of Rachel and Heather's hobbies is sculpture so although the decoration is traditional – wooden floors, pretty curtains, good furniture, family portraits – there are glimpses of well-travelled bohemianism. The dining room is iron-oxide red, there are tapestries from Ecuador and Peru, and vibrant colours glow in comfortable bedrooms. Pretty bathrooms sparkle with unusual tiles and original ceramic sinks, and there are long views from deep window seats. Charmingly relaxing and easy-going.

Price	From £60.
Rooms	1 double.
Meals	Pubs within 0.25 miles.
Closed	November–March.
Directions	From A38 Exeter to Plymouth road towards Bovey Tracey. Follow signs to Widecombe, Keep The Old Inn on right; house is on left after 50 yds.

Rachel Belgrave & Heather Garner
The Old Rectory,
Widecombe in the Moor TQ13 7TB

Tel	01364 621231
Fax	01364 621231
Email	rachel.belgrave@care4free.net

Entry 28   Map 2

The Old Rectory

The garden: The house is covered in wisteria and climbing roses, and looks out over mature trees planted 150 years ago: a lovely setting for this three-acre garden with smooth lawns. Copper beech, a rare and large maple, Californian spruce, elms and yews rub shoulders with more recent additions: magnolia, Japanese maple and hundreds of rhododendrons and fruit trees. Wander down the limestone terracing and steps to find a spot by the Victorian grotto and watch for carp in the deep pond, admire the changing sculptures, play a game of croquet. Or just head for the saltwater, solar-heated pool with smart decking and enjoy the view with a sundowner. There's a pretty parterre with box and lavender from which stem obelisks with white roses, while romantic paths have been cut through the wildflowers and grasses, and gazebos hold up some very old and scented roses. The orchard is humming with apples, pears and plums, rescued chickens strut through it and you will meet some lop-eared rabbits who have their home here. Wildlife is abundant and you may even hear a screech owl. The vegetable garden is organic and provides much for the table, the meadow is dotted with sheep. All very English and Leonie and Laurence make it look so effortless!

The house: In the pretty village but protected by high walls, this early Victorian house has beautiful features, and Leonie has made the inside sing with a stylish makeover. Great for big house parties, there's a games room with a full-size snooker table, a large sitting room with books and plenty of sofas, and a dining room with a long table. Light floods in from huge windows. Sweep up the staircase to rather grand and plentiful bedrooms, some sumptuous, some minimalist, all spacious and with fresh and lovely bathrooms. Breakfast is a treat and served on the terrace in summer overlooking the wooded valley.

Price	£70-£120. Singles £63-£108.
Rooms	6: 4 doubles, 2 four-posters.
Meals	Pub 200 yds.
Closed	Christmas & New Year.
Directions	Past Red Lion Hotel, through main street. Left at the old blue pump, gates to house facing you.

Leonie Nanassy & Laurence Delamar
The Old Rectory,
Fore Street Hill, Chulmleigh EX18 7BS
Tel   01769 580123
Email   therectory@nanassy.com
Web   www.theoldrectorychulmleigh.co.uk

The Priory

The garden: Dawn calls the Priory gardens Luffendlic Stede: 'lovely place' in Old English. It extends to about an acre around the house, then slopes gently down to the village pond. Romance is definitely the theme in the 'hortus conclusus', a medieval courtly love garden with a turf seat, enclosed by a chestnut trellis covered in roses and old herbs. At the front, Dawn is planting three Tudor knot gardens that demonstrate how knot gardens have developed; at the back, an apothecary's garden with a rose cloister and a replica medieval font with slate rills, surrounded by deep beds planted with scented flowers – roses, lavender, honeysuckle and lilies. The Textile Garden is filled with plants connected to either the designs on tapestries and embroideries, or the dyes, fibres and tools used to produce them. The orchard is being planted with old varieties of fruit trees (Devonshire Quarrenden, Court Pendue Platt) underplanted with wildflowers, and the raised vegetable beds are a celebration of organic companion planting. Three hundred native trees and plants have been planted in the first season alone, including willow, hazel, black poplar, limes. Wildlife includes kingfishers, bats and woodpeckers. A garden full of promise.

The house: Right beside the main street in the village – but the full impact of this stunning house doesn't hit you until you are inside. Dating from 1154 it was originally an Augustine priory; now Dawn has swept through with a fresh broom while keeping all the lovely architectural features – there's even a 30-foot well in the drawing room. Bedrooms are spoiling and peaceful with deep mattresses on large beds with organic cotton sheets, herbs and fresh flowers; bathrooms are sumptuous. Dawn runs courses in textiles, food history and gardens. You are incredibly well looked after here.

Price	£150. Singles £90.
Rooms	2 doubles.
Meals	Light supper, 2 courses, £25. Dinner, 4 courses, £40. Restaurant 8 miles.
Closed	Rarely.
Directions	Leave M5 at junc. 27. Immediately take 1st exit signed Sampford Peverell/Halberton. Continue to Halberton. House is on left within 2nd set of traffic calming.

Dawn Riggs
The Priory,
Halberton EX16 7AF

Tel	01884 821234
Email	dawn@theprioryhalberton.co.uk
Web	www.theprioryhalberton.co.uk

 Travel Club Offer. See page 290.

🎔 🔊 ⮌

Regency House

The garden: Jenny was in the middle of her horticultural and garden design courses at Bicton when she moved here, so she put her increasing knowledge to immediate good use as she licked the jungle she had bought into shape. The large south-facing walled kitchen garden is old and beautiful and has been brought back into full production; nowadays Jenny rarely buys vegetables. Plum trees are fanned against the wall, and at the top a bench looks down a central espaliered apple walk. On the other side of the house an artistic son's fern sculpture attracts admiring comments, and nearby Jenny has planted a colourful bog garden around a little dew pond. However, her favourite area remains her spring garden by the drive with its *Anemone blanda* and bulbs, *Exochorda macrantha* and epimediums – an astonishing array of plants. There's restoration work going on along the fast-moving stream where a mid-19th century race and waterfall are being rebuilt. Further upstream the drive passes through a newly cobbled ford, which already looks 200 years old. It's a bit like the Good Life at Regency House: not only the garden interests her visitors but also her horses, little Dexter cattle and Jacob sheep. *NGS.*

The house: Beautiful proportions at this 1855 rectory, with varnished floors and rugs downstairs. Both the music room with grand piano (you are welcome to play) and the drawing room have floor-to-ceiling windows overlooking the lake and the garden. Jenny and her husband hunt locally so there are hunting prints around; interesting contemporary paintings too, and plenty of books. The large, light bedroom is decorated in classic pale colours and keeps its original shutters. Enjoy bread from the Aga and eggs from the hens at breakfast in the huge farmhouse kitchen. Best in summer – and the walking is marvellous.

Price	£90. Singles £45.
Rooms	1 twin with separate bathroom.
Meals	Dinner £25. Pub 3 miles.
Closed	Rarely.
Directions	M5 junc. 26 for Wellington, from north. Left at roundabout; immed. right at junction, left at next junction. Right at top of hill. Left at x-roads. In Hemyock take Dunkeswell/Honiton Road. House 500 yds on right.

Mrs Jenny Parsons
Regency House,
Hemyock, Cullompton EX15 3RQ
Tel   01823 680238
Email   jenny.parsons@btinternet.com

Travel Club Offer. See page 290.

Applebarn Cottage

The garden: Before even setting foot in the house, the Spencers knew this was the place for them. The grounds and outlook were irresistible. Though it had become a wilderness, the garden had obviously once been well designed and stocked, and the views... on a clear day you can see Lamberts Castle and even, with binoculars, watch cricket matches on the village green. Exploring the garden is a delight, not only because of its varied nature but also because of the intoxicating scents. (Birds and butterflies seem to love it too.) In front of the house is a two-level terrace. On the upper level – a lovely place to dine on summer evenings – grow *Magnolia stellata*, Irish yew, camellias, roses and a fine show of hellebores. Lower down are more camellias, scented clarydendron and euchryphia, yucca and huge flax features. Paths and gently sloping lawns lead to a secret, paved garden, guarded by bamboos threaded through with 'Albertine' and other roses. At its heart is a two-tiered Italian fountain, surrounded by Chinese lilac and ferns; nearby stands a splendid 'wedding cake' tree. Gunnera, royal ferns and euphorbia reign supreme in the bog gardens, while the woody wild garden has magnolias, broom and monkey puzzles. And in the spring, endless drifts of primroses.

The house: A tree-lined drive leads to a long white wall; a gate in the wall opens to an explosion of colour – the garden. Come for a deliciously restful place and the nicest hosts. The wisteria-covered 17th-century cottage is full of books, flowers and paintings, and bedrooms are large, traditional and wonderfully comfortable, with all-white bathrooms. One of the rooms is in an extension but blends in beautifully. Breakfast, served in a lovely slate-floored dining room, includes a neighbour's homemade honey. Eat in if you can: dinner is superb and includes vegetables and fruits from the garden.

Price	£74-£80. (Half-board option.)
Rooms	2 suites.
Meals	Dinner, 3 courses, £26.
	Pub/restaurant 3 miles.
Closed	Last two weeks November to 1 March.
Directions	A30 from Chard, signed Honiton. Left at top of hill signed Wambrook & Stockland. After 3 miles pass Ferne Animal Sanctuary. Straight on at next x-roads (Membury); 0.75 miles, left, signed Cotley/Ridge. Past Hartshill Boarding Kennels; signed 2nd right.

Patricia & Robert Spencer
Applebarn Cottage, Bewley Down,
Membury, Axminster EX13 7JX

Tel	01460 220873
Fax	01460 220873
Email	paspenceruk@yahoo.co.uk
Web	www.applebarn-cottage.co.uk

 Travel Club Offer. See page 290.

Lytchett Hard

The garden: One fascinating acre adjoins a reeded inlet of Poole harbour plus their own SSSI where, if you're lucky, you'll spot a Dartford Warbler among the gorse. The garden has been created from scratch over the past 30 years and carefully designed to make the most of the views over heathland – haunt of two species of lizard – and water. Liz is a trained horticulturist and she and David have capitalised on the mild weather here to grow tender plants; copious additions of compost and horse manure have improved the sandy soil. These tender treasures thrive gloriously and are unusually large – you're greeted by a huge phormium in the pretty entrance garden by the drive; the terrace is a stone and gravel Mediterranean garden. Acid-lovers are happy, so there are fine displays of camellias and rhododendrons among hosts of daffodil and tulips once the sweeps of snowdrops have finished. Three borders are colour-themed, each representing a wedding anniversary: silver, pearl and ruby. Play croquet on the large lawn, explore the private woodland where David has created winding paths, relax in the shade of the gazebo or in the warmth of the working conservatory, admire the many unusual plants, or simply sit back and enjoy that shimmering view. *RHS. Plants for sale in aid of Dorset Wildlife Trust.*

The house: The house takes its name from the place where fishermen brought their craft ashore, in the unspoilt upper reaches of Poole harbour. The three guest bedrooms – the four-poster is the largest – all face south and make the most of the main garden below and the views beyond. Elizabeth and David's green fingers conjure up a mass of home-grown produce as well as flowers – vegetables, jams, herbs and fruit. Guests can linger in the antique oak dining room, or breakfast on the terrace on warm days; there are log fires and a lovely, huggable pointer called Coco. *Minimum stay two nights at weekends & July / August.*

Price	£65–£90. Singles from £50.
Rooms	3: 1 twin, 1 double, 1 four-poster.
Meals	Pub 1 mile.
Closed	Occasionally.
Directions	From Upton x-roads (0.5 miles SE of A35/A350 interchange), west into Dorchester Rd; 2nd left into Seaview Rd; cross junc. over Sandy Lane into Slough Lane; immed. 1st left into Beach Rd. 150 yds on, on right.

David & Elizabeth Collinson
Lytchett Hard,
Beach Road, Upton, Poole BH16 5NA

| Tel | 01202 622297 |
| Email | lytchetthard@ntlworld.com |

Entry 33   Map 3

Higher Melcombe Manor

The garden: Come for the far-reaching views over Blackmore Vale towards Somerset: these two acres appear to blend quite effortlessly into the countryside, and Highland cattle are sometimes seen grazing in the pastures. At the front of the house there are sweeping lawns, a shrubbery woodland area and a deep herbaceous bank, its flowers tumbling over each other in waves of yellow rudbeckia, white stocks and pink sedums. Stroll along paths through the shrubby glade, where the dappled shade of an enormous copper beech creates the perfect spot for hellebores in spring and hemerocallis in summer; the tall blue spires of verbena soften the formality of clipped yew topiary hedges and open lawns. To the west of the house are island beds crammed with goodies, including towering hollyhocks, purple eryngiums and pink peonies. Here is a hidden pond and fountain and more little paths, bordered by lavender, which lead to a south-facing wall covered with climbing roses, clematis and figs. Near the entrance to the house and chapel Lorel is making changes and introducing some special scented roses. Benches are dotted about and there are seating areas to east and west for sunny mornings and spectacular sunsets.

The house: You will feel charmed by this manor house of local stone; some of the rooms date back to 1570. The sitting room has fine mullioned windows, the Great Hall is magnificent with a stained-glass window, and the dining room has a log fire and a long oak table. The first bedroom is very traditional with dark panelling, rich fabrics, a grand stone fireplace and a bathroom along the corridor; leap into the 21st century in the attic where two stylish rooms have plenty of pizazz and a little sitting room between them. Lorel and Michael are still working on this huge inherited project, worth a visit for its history alone. *Smoking allowed in parts of the house.*

Price	£75–£95. Singles from £60.
Rooms	3: 2 doubles; 1 double with separate bath.
Meals	Pub 1.5 miles.
Closed	Christmas.
Directions	From Dorchester, A35 then take Piddlehinton exit (B3142). First left to Cheselbourne, then first right into Long Lane. Continue for 5 miles until crossroads at Melcombe Bingham, turn left, signed 'Private Road to Higher Melcombe'.

Lorel Morton & Michael Woodhouse
Higher Melcombe Manor,
Melcombe Bingham DT2 7PB

Tel	01258 880251
Email	lorel@lorelmorton.com

Polemonium Plantery

The garden: Hard to believe that this whole area was once a concrete dog run, surrounded by block paving; David and Dianne now hold the National Plant Collections of Polemonium, Gilia and Hakonechloa. Scented plants abound and the cottage garden is planted in themes of purple and pink, then yellow and blue. The area was first excavated, then improved and planted over winter to be ready in time for their first open day in May. Now the house is surrounded by a north-facing cottage garden with rare trees, shrubs and herbaceous plants, an alpine garden with troughs and raised beds, and a narrow winter garden with a pergola leading to the secret garden – a south-facing gravel area with scented plants. There are lots of seating areas and guests can have afternoon tea or a late breakfast in the secret garden by the fountain water feature. Rare trees include a *Sorbus aucuparia* and a *Chionanthus virginicus*, all underplanted with shrubs and trillions of bulbs for spring and winter interest. Wildlife is abundant and most of the soft fruit and vegetables end up on your plate, fully organic. Green-fingered David and Dianne are totally committed.

The house: The approach is mixed countryside – this was all coal mining country – and you will find the house behind the back of the village school: a 1950s building, modernised and enlarged in the 90s. David and Dianne are greener than a cabbage and deeply keen on their garden and allotment, and looking after you – rather well. Bedrooms are spotlessly clean and unfussy, with good firm beds, feather and down bedding covered in organic cotton and hand-made rugs in organic wool; bathrooms are functional but up to date, with organic soap. Food is organic, of course, dinner is a treat and all is homemade. Good value.

Price	£56. Singles £28.
Rooms	3: 1 single; 1 double, 1 single sharing bath (let to same party only).
Meals	Dinner £12. Packed lunch £3. Pub 0.5 miles.
Closed	Never.
Directions	7 miles east of Durham City on A181. South into Trimdon Grange on B1278. House opposite green behind village school. Good public transport links – No. 55 from Durham City, 2 miles. West of National Cycle Route 1.

David & Dianne Nichol-Brown
Polemonium Plantery,
28 Sunnyside Terrace, Trimdon Grange,
Trimdon Station TS29 6HF

Tel	01429 881529
Email	bandb@polemonium.co.uk
Web	www.polemonium.co.uk

Entry 35   Map 6

Mount Hall

The garden: The drive sweeps you around and up to the handsome pillared and stuccoed front porch of Mount Hall, overlooking a wide lawn flanked by mature trees and shrubs. Sue has a great interest in trees and the many well-established varieties act as a dramatic backdrop to the labour-saving foliage plants which speak for themselves through their different shapes and shades of green and yellow. This is a place for retreat, very tranquil, with plenty of seats under trees, or by the pool. The walled pool garden is totally secluded and private, a haven of peace watched over by a huge eucalyptus; Sue prefers calm, cool and subdued colours in her planting. A beautiful evergreen tapestry border is of year-round interest in muted greens; elsewhere greys and whites, pale blues and silver predominate, most of the plants coming from the Beth Chatto Gardens eight miles away. The pool was an erstwhile swimming pool: the formal rectangular shape has been kept, but now teems with wildlife. Nicknamed her "gosh" pool after her visitors' first reactions, the fish and frogs have bred and multiplied well since its conversion. So peaceful, four miles from the edge of the Dedham Vale, and close to the oldest recorded town of Colchester. *HPS.*

The house: An elegant, Queen Anne listed house. Upstairs rooms in the house are large, light, quietly faded and deeply comfortable, with garden views. For those who prefer independence, or those in wheelchairs, the ground-floor annexe is a good space, with twin beds, futons for families, a huge sofa, good books and its own door out to a separate garden for visiting pooches. Bathrooms are old-fashioned but spotless, there's a sitting room for guests with a bridge table and homemade jams for breakfast. Set out from this peaceful place to explore Constable country – and the Beth Chatto Gardens. *Dogs welcome to sleep in the annexe.*

Price	£80. Singles £45.
Rooms	3: 1 twin, 1 single. Annexe: 1 twin/double, 2 futons.
Meals	Pub 1 mile.
Closed	Rarely.
Directions	A134 through Great Horkesley to Rose & Crown pub, left (London Rd). 1st left marked West Bergholt; 2nd drive on left.

Sue Carbutt
Mount Hall, Great Horkesley,
Colchester CO6 4BZ

Tel	01206 271359
Email	suecarbutt@yahoo.co.uk

Ivydene House

The garden: When Rosemary and Pete arrived 12 years ago they inherited a two-acre expanse of mud, weeds, stones and rubble. Since then everything, apart from a pretty sprinkling of old apple trees, has been planned and planted by the Gallaghers. Flanked on two sides by farmland, divided by a vast shrub-filled island bed, this garden is gorgeously, unpreciously informal. The most formal part is to one side – huge bed, pristine lavender walk, smooth lawn and yew-hedge archway leading to a pond with a water feature and pergola. The pond is surrounded by water-loving plants and is left alone to encourage wildlife – rest awhile and watch the moorhens flit in and out of the rushes. Or take a picnic and a rug to the lawn. Interesting trees like robinia, elder and eucalyptus are dotted about, and there's a pretty row of hydrangea 'Annabel'. The wilder other side of the garden is where mown paths swoop through a wood of 300 English trees, surrounded by a hawthorn hedge and with a trampoline in the middle. The lovely south-facing terrace with a Mediterranean feel has more seating areas; a sunny conservatory hugs the house. This is a young garden worth emulating – for its easy informality and its subtle, country-garden colours.

The house: A joy to arrive and a pleasure to stay, at this red-brick 1790s house a short hop from the Malvern Hills. Rosemary greets guests with tea and homemade cake by the fire, little Teddie (white and fluffy) shows you around the garden. Downstairs has been decorated in warm farmhouse style: old polished quarry tiles, cream walls, fresh flowers, wicker dining chairs, a great big inglenook. Fabulous bedrooms have an upbeat elegance with contemporary headboards, crisp linen and silk cushions – "just heavenly," say readers. Bathrooms sparkle, breakfasts are beautiful and Peter and Rosemary couldn't be nicer. Such value.

Price	From £70. Singles from £45.
Rooms	2: 1 twin/double, 1 double.
Meals	Pub within walking distance.
Closed	Christmas.
Directions	M5 junc. 8 onto M50. Exit junc. 1 onto A38 north, then 1st left to Ripple. Through to Uckinghall, over bridge, house at bottom on right.

Rosemary Gallagher
Ivydene House,
Uckinghall, Tewkesbury GL20 6ES

Tel	01684 592453
Email	rosemaryg@fsmail.net
Web	www.ivydenehouse.net

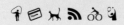 Travel Club Offer. See page 290.

Lower Farm House

The garden: Borders here are seasonal and colour themed: white and blue in early spring, red and yellow going into summer when things get hot and frothy with penstemons, delphiniums, roses and lavender. There's a huge terrace where you can sit and admire the setting sun, or wander past the pond and into woodland to watch the evening flight of birds over the spring-fed lake. Although these two acres of garden have evolved gradually since Zelie and Nicholas started from scratch, when they moved here in 1991, they are maturing fast. The result is an open and flowing country garden to complement the long and lovely views and the soft stone of well-maintained walls that provide a wonderful backdrop to the many climbers, including clematis and honeysuckle. Other good structure comes from fine pleached hornbeam and yew hedges. Mown paths lead to Zelie's flourishing vegetable garden; if you choose to eat in, you'll reap the rewards of her labours at dinner. The next project is underway and the picture is continually evolving. A gently restful, and supremely comfortable place to round off the day after taking in other Cotswold charmers; Hidcote, Kiftsgate and Bourton are close by and on the urban front Cheltenham, Stratford, and Oxford.

The house: Jane Austen used to stay in Adlestrop and Fanny would surely have found it 'most agreeable' and chosen kedgeree for breakfast. Once the Home Farm of the Leigh estate, Lower Farm House has a perfect Georgian feel – high ceilings, sash windows, and well-proportioned rooms graciously furnished yet not dauntingly formal. Nicholas and Zelie are both charming and articulate and love entertaining. Their pale-carpeted guest bedrooms are softly serene with fine garden views. Meals – everything as organic and locally sourced as possible – sound superb; cooking and gardening are Zelie's passions.

Price	£96–£104. Singles £68.
Rooms	3: 1 double, 2 twins/doubles.
Meals	Dinner, 3 courses, £30. Pubs/restaurants 1.5 miles.
Closed	Rarely.
Directions	A436 from Stow; after 3 miles, left to Adlestrop; right at T-junc.; after double bend drive 50 yds on right; sign at end of drive. Map on website.

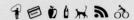 Travel Club Offer. See page 290.

Nicholas & Zelie Mason
Lower Farm House, Adlestrop,
Stow-on-the-Wold GL56 0YR

Tel	01608 658756, 01608 658700
Fax	01608 659458
Email	info@adlestrop-lowerfarm.com
Web	www.adlestrop-lowerfarm.com

Entry 38   Map 3

Clapton Manor

The garden: James abandoned his life in the City in order to garden. Now he runs his own garden tours business and lectures extensively for NADFAS and the NACF, as well as designing gardens with his wife Karin. They have created a delightfully informal garden here, with a formal touch or two: a perspective path between the double borders; a pyramid of Portuguese laurel with pruned Moorish 'doors'. The gently sloping garden wraps itself around the lovely old manor house and is divided into compartments defined by ancient Cotswold stone walls and hedges of yew, hornbeam, box and cotoneaster. And there's a wildflower meadow with its own mound from which you can survey the surrounding hills. The garden is planned for year-round interest, with sparkling displays of rare snowdrops, narcissi and hellebores in winter and spring. Summer sees masses of old roses climbing through trees, over arches and in the tiny orchard; garden flowers (never florists'!) fill the rooms. This is a lovingly designed garden in an immensely quiet village where B&B guests can relax and enjoy a fine collection of plants in a beautiful setting. Nothing disturbs the peace except birdsong.

The house: Karin and James's 16th-century manor is as all homes should be: loved and lived-in. And, with three-foot-thick walls, flagstoned floors, sit-in fireplaces and stone-mullioned windows, it's gorgeous. The enclosed garden, full of birdsong and roses, wraps itself around the house. One bedroom has a secret door that leads to a fuchsia-pink bathroom; the other room, smaller, is wallpapered in a honeysuckle trellis and has wonderful garden views. Wellies, dogs, barbours, log fires… and breakfast by a vast Tudor fireplace on homemade bread and jams and eggs from the hens. A happy, charming family home.

Price	From £95. Singles £85.
Rooms	2: 1 double, 1 twin/double.
Meals	Pub/restaurants within 15-minute drive.
Closed	Rarely.
Directions	A429 Cirencester-Stow. Right signed Sherborne & Clapton. In village, pass grassy area to left, postbox in one corner; house straight ahead on left on corner.

Karin & James Bolton
Clapton Manor,
Clapton-on-the-Hill GL54 2LG

Tel	01451 810202
Email	bandb@claptonmanor.co.uk
Web	www.claptonmanor.co.uk

Drakestone House

The garden: The hauntingly atmospheric Edwardian landscaped grounds would make a perfect setting for open-air Shakespeare – rather apposite since it's said that young Shakespeare roamed the hills around Stinchcombe. Hugh's grandparents laid out the grounds, influenced by a love of Italian gardens and admiration for Gertrude Jekyll. When Hugh and Crystal moved here, the garden was distressed and needed attention, particularly the magnificent topiary. The beautifully varied, lofty, sculptural yew and box hedges, domes and busbies dominating the view from the house are restored to perfection, creating a series of garden rooms with a backdrop of woodland. Paths and a romantic Irish yew walk invite you to wander as you move from one compartment to the next. By the house, a pergola is covered with wisteria in spring and rambling roses in summer, near displays of lovely old roses underplanted with lavender. Crystal describes these two acres as informally formal or formally informal – she can't quite decide which. But it's that elegant Edwardian design with its Mediterranean mood that makes Drakestone House so special. The best moments to enjoy the grounds are on sunny days when the shadows play strange tricks with the sculptured hedges and trees... expect Puck or Ariel to make a dramatic entrance at any moment!

The house: Utterly delightful people with wide-ranging interests (ex-British Council and college lecturing; arts, travel, gardening...) in a manor-type house full of beautiful furniture. A treat. The house was born of the Arts and Crafts movement and remains fascinating: wood panels painted green, a log-fired drawing-room for guests, quarry tiles on window sills, handsome old furniture, comfortable proportions... elegant but human, refined but easy. And the garden's massive clipped hedges are superb.

Price	£78. Singles £49.
Rooms	3: 1 twin/double, 1 double, 1 twin, all with separate bath/shower.
Meals	Dinner £25. BYO. Pub/restaurant under 1 mile.
Closed	Never.
Directions	B4060 from Stinchcombe to Wotton-under-Edge. 0.25 miles out of Stinchcombe village. Driveway on left marked, before long bend.

Hugh & Crystal Mildmay
Drakestone House,
Stinchcombe, Dursley GL11 6AS

Tel	01453 542140
Fax	01453 542140

Winforton Court

The garden: A delightful little walled garden greets you, its path edged with profuse purple and green sage studded with perennial geraniums. When Jackie arrived, all the grounds were down to grass with some mature trees and with fine views across the Wye Valley to the Black Mountains – there's a lovely walk to the river. She took heaps of cuttings from her previous home, created borders, planted vigorously and transformed her big new garden. The sunny courtyard behind the house has a fruit-covered fig tree and mature magnolia, flowering shrubs in containers, cherubs on walls and a fountain brought from Portugal. Beyond lies her open, terraced garden dominated by a weeping willow, with an ancient standing stone on a ley line shaded by a tall horse chestnut, emerald lawns, flower-packed beds and, below, a stream and small water garden. She has even planted the edge of the parking area with colourful sun-lovers thrusting through the gravel. Jackie aimed to make a garden to complement Winforton Court's dreamy architecture, and that's what she has achieved. Guests love it here – regulars come bearing gifts to add to her collection, and are sometimes generously given cuttings so a little bit of Winforton Court will grow in their garden and give them pleasure for years to come.

The house: The staircase, mentioned in Pevsner's, is 17th century. Most of this half-timbered house was built in 1500 and is breathtaking in its ancient dignity, its undulating floors, its wonderful thick walls and its great oak beams. The beamed long gallery is perfect for celebrations or big family dinners. Take a book from the small library and settle into a window seat overlooking the gardens. There is a guest sitting room too, festooned with works of art by local artists. The two four-postered bedrooms verge on the luxurious; so does the double, and all have fruit juice and sherry. Gorgeous.

Price	£80–£100. Singles from £65.
Rooms	3: 1 double, 1 four-poster, 1 four-poster suite.
Meals	Pub/restaurant 2-minute walk.
Closed	Christmas.
Directions	From Hereford, A438 into village. On left with a green sign & iron gates.

Jackie Kingdon
Winforton Court,
Winforton HR3 6EA

Tel	01544 328498
Fax	01544 328498
Web	www.winfortoncourt.co.uk

 Travel Club Offer. See page 290.

Entry 41   Map 2

Brobury House

The garden: Enthusiastic, energetic Pru and Keith are passionate about these gardens that sweep down to the Wye, and have won Green Tourism and Wildlife Action awards for their work. Together with designer Peter Antonius, they are continuing to expand and develop the graceful tree-filled terraces, laid out in the 1880s to make the most of the views. Open to the public (hence the car park at the front and the green signs), this spectacular waterside setting has plenty to explore and places in which to sit and muse. Close to the house the grounds are formal: a south-facing lawn, an acacia-shaded lily pond and a Lutyens-inspired pool with parterre, all overlooking more lawns, and copper beeches, lavender, climbing roses and clipped hornbeam hedges. Rose beds, magnolias, asters and dahlias zing with colour around a pretty pergola and a dramatic Bodmin standing stone. The grounds were once part of a large kitchen garden and vegetables flourish in the original Victorian greenhouses. At the outer reaches, formal gardens give way to the wild, with a natural pond, a mature orchard and a fern garden. The river views take in the church, the ice house and the rectory on the opposite bank where Kilvert lived and is buried. Wildlife thrives on the riverbank: kingfishers are common and you may even spot an otter.

The house: Here are emerald-green riverbanks, and a huge handsome house dominated by a wisteria-cloaked folly. The ancient mulberry tree on the lawn was planted by Victorian diarist Francis Kilvert, who lived across the river. Super big bedrooms with traditional wallpapers, polished furniture and carpeted floors have country or garden views – and it's a short dash to the twins' smart shower rooms. After a perfect night's sleep, tuck into locally sourced organic breakfasts on the terrace or in the conservatory – light and lovely, with comfortable seating. Conveniently close to bookish, eccentric Hay-on-Wye, and the Tudor village of Weobley.

Price	From £60. Singles from £45.
Rooms	3: 1 double; 1 twin, 1 twin/double each with separate shower.
Meals	Pub 2.5 miles.
Closed	Christmas, New Year & occasionally.
Directions	Turn south off A438, 10 miles west of Hereford, signed 'Bredwardine & Brobury'. Continue 1 mile. House on left before bridge. Parking for visitors.

Pru Cartwright
Brobury House,
Brobury, Bredwardine HR3 6BS

Tel	01981 500229
Email	enquiries@broburyhouse.co.uk
Web	www.broburyhouse.co.uk

Travel Club Offer. See page 290.

Ethical Collection: Environment; Food. See page 294.

The Old Rectory

The garden: Jenny loves her 'mini-Heligan': three secluded acres at the foot of the Black Mountains. She and Chrix spent months hacking through the undergrowth to uncover lost paths and plants; now the sloping wilderness of long grasses and brambles is unrecognisable. Mature trees – conifers, oak, ash and acacias – provide the backdrop to well-tended lawns and large beds filled to bursting with a variety of plants of many colours. There's a pond, home to newts and frogs, where irises and king cups flourish, a lovingly tended croquet lawn and a summer house that rotates on the upper terrace. The old rectory has some well-pruned roses scrambling up it, and great views of the surrounding countryside from that terrace giving a wonderful feeling of space – in spite of the tall trees. Plenty of evergreens give joy in winter, with roses like 'Kiftsgate' clambering up them, creating quite a display in spring and summer. Huge swathes of lawn are left unmown to protect spring bulbs like daffodils, jonquils and fritillaries. Intentionally leaving some areas untouched has earned the Juckes a wildlife award from the Herefordshire Nature Trust. This garden reflects the character of its owners: relaxed, informal, thoroughly engaging.

The house: A Georgian rectory in the 'golden valley' where Wales and England converge – perfect for walkers. Inside, an unpretentious home: stags' heads, family portraits, stuffed birds and Milly the sweet spaniel. Bedrooms are large, airy and filled with good furniture, books, and big windows for garden views; the feel is not luxurious but most comfortable. There's an elegant drawing room with a grand piano that you are welcome to play, a dining room with a long table and French windows that open to the garden on balmy days. Chrix and Jenny are delightful people and the pub is a mere stroll.

Price	From £60. Singles from £35.
Rooms	3: 1 double, 1 twin/double; 1 twin/double with separate bath.
Meals	Pubs in village 4-minute walk.
Closed	Rarely.
Directions	A465 to Abergavenny. 12 miles from Hereford, right on B4347. After 1.5 miles, left into village, then right by Temple Bar Pub. Left at top of road (School Road). House 1st on right.

Jenny Juckes
The Old Rectory,
Ewyas Harold HR2 0TX

Tel	01981 240498
Fax	01981 240498
Email	jenny.juckes@btopenworld.com
Web	www.theoldrectory.org.uk

Entry 43   Map 2

Dippersmoor Manor

The garden: Robinia, catalpa, rowan and tulip trees dot the main lawn, buzzards float overhead and owls and bats roost in the barn. This big, secluded, hillside garden, with wonderful views to the Black Mountains, was virtually a field when Amanda and Hexie arrived 25 years ago. It was they who planted the avenue of poplars curving up to the house. A flagstone path leads you through a knot garden to the door, overhung by a vine which has been there since the 1920s. Roses, wisteria, quince and hydrangea scramble haphazardly up the walls and everywhere there are things to engage the eye. At the centre of a terraced lawn stands a stone cider press brimming with plants; next door is a box-hedged rose garden. More roses, lavender and sweet peas scent a square, pretty garden in front of the stone summer house, where swallows nest. (You can play table tennis here too.) The old stables provide a good backdrop to a bright border and pleached limes screen off an area destined to be a vegetable garden. Old cider orchards and a bluebell wood are fine places to explore, a pergola festooned with vines and clematis provides dappled shade – just the place to sit with a drink.

The house: Dating in parts back to the 15th century, the red sandstone house is flanked by a magnificent brick and timber long barn. The bedrooms are traditional, airy and spacious with crisp white linen and views to woodland and pasture towards the south, and mountains to the west. Breakfast is in the dining room, where the fireplace was once used for curing bacon, or out under the pergola; on warm evenings, dinners of local produce and homegrown vegetables can be taken outside under the vine in candlelit privacy, or with the charming Hexie and Amanda.

Price	From £80. Singles from £50.
Rooms	3: 1 double, 1 twin; 1 double with separate bathroom.
Meals	Dinner £18-£25 by arrangement. Pub 3 miles.
Closed	Rarely.
Directions	Turn left 7 miles south of Hereford on A465 to Kilpeck. Through village past Red Lion pub. Fork left on sharp bend signed village hall. Turn right over cattle grid 100 yds past village hall up a poplar-lined drive.

Hexie & Amanda Millais
Dippersmoor Manor,
Kilpeck HR2 9DW

Tel	01981 570209
Email	hmm@dippersmoor.eclipse.co.uk
Web	www.dippersmoor.com

Hall End House

The garden: It is an especial treat for garden lovers to visit a garden in the making – particularly one with plans as ambitious as those that Angela is developing with the help of a talented young designer (Josie Anderson from Cheltenham). What was once a run-down farmyard is being transformed into a large, open, elegant, feature-packed garden, that perfectly complements the grand listed Georgian farmhouse that Angela and Hugh have restored so brilliantly. A neglected pond at the front has been cleared and planted with water-loving beauties; a second has been created nearby so that as you approach up the drive you see the house in reflection. And so much to enjoy once you arrive: a designer kitchen garden, a herb garden, a formal rose garden with the finest roses, a croquet lawn to add greenness and space. Angela loves flowers and her beds and borders are brimming with the loveliest plants. There's a tennis court for the energetic, a summer house in which to unwind and a large conservatory – relax and gaze at the splendours outside. On a sunny day, take a dip in the striking, L-shaped (heated) pool lined in deepest blue. The setting, in 500 acres of farmland, is a delight: views everywhere – of woodland, open countryside and parkland – and one of the loveliest corners of Herefordshire.

The house: All the grandeur you could ask for from the moment you enter. The airy hall has a handsome staircase leading to wide landings and the bedrooms upstairs. They are large and elegant, with rich curtains, comfortable beds and immaculate new bath/shower rooms. The dining and drawing rooms echo the mood of classic English elegance. A friendly welcome from a couple who have devoted an enormous amount of care and energy to the restoration of both house and garden. Lamb and other produce from this extremely well-managed farm is used when in season. *Children over 12 welcome.*

Price	£95–£120. Singles £60.
Rooms	3: 1 double, 1 twin, 1 four-poster.
Meals	Dinner (winter only), 3 courses plus coffee and chocolates, £25. BYO wine. Pub/restaurant 2.5 miles.
Closed	Christmas & New Year.
Directions	From Ledbury A449 Ross-on-Wye road to Much Marcle. Turn right between garage and stores. Right after 300 yds signed Rushall and Kynaston. After 2.5 miles, drive is on left.

Angela & Hugh Jefferson
Hall End House,
Kynaston, Ledbury HR8 2PD

Tel	01531 670225
Fax	01531 670747
Email	khjefferson@hallend91.freeserve.co.uk
Web	www.hallendhouse.com

 Travel Club Offer. See page 290.

Entry 45   Map 2

Homestead Farm

The garden: Lake, boathouse and island – enchanting. A sunken garden, too, vegetable garden that is a delight, a field with a folly, mown paths, windbreak trees and fabulous long views. All this has been created by Iain and Joanna, who arrived clutching some pots from their old home in Scotland. It began with the flagstoned and fountain'd terrace. Along paths and across the garden are mounded metal arches laced with roses and clematis, a rope swag (once the Mallaig ferry's rope) smothered in 'Prince Charles' clematis and bushes of white *spinosissima* roses. There's a honeysuckle hedge, two greenhouse with a fanned nectarine and peach, abundant vines, a fruit cage with 'Autumn Bliss' raspberries and wild strawberries grown from seed. The field is mown with paths, cut for hay in the autumn, and contains hundreds of trees planted for the millennium; some as a shelter belt, some in avenues. Iain's "folly" is a circle of pleached rowans with a stockade of 20 young oaks donated by the architect to replace those felled for the house. Views are created everywhere and across the length of the field towards the lake there's an avenue of *Malus coronaria* 'Charlottae' alternating with bird cherries. And 2,000 snowdrops have been planted with wild daffodils and a carpet of bluebells. *RHS*.

The house: A stunning mixture of old and new. The new oak-framed barn is joined to a 16th-century keeper's cottage and all is light, airy and timbered. Joanna is creative in her use of colour, there are prints, paintings, books, an open fireplace and a gorgeous drawing room. Bedrooms have pale green carpeting, crisp white linen and dazzling light; one bathroom is in the bedroom. A veranda outside and balcony above cunningly melt a 500-year age difference into nothing at all, views reach over cider orchards and hops and Lulu the Tibetan spaniel's welcome is as genuine as your hostess's. *Teenagers & babes in arms welcome.*

Price	From £80. Singles £45.
Rooms	2: 1 double, 1 twin.
Meals	Pubs/restaurants 3 miles.
Closed	Christmas, New Year & occasionally.
Directions	A438 towards Hereford from Ledbury, north on A417 for 2 miles. At UK garage right to Canon Frome. After 0.75 miles, right in front of red brick gates of Rochester House; house 0.5 miles at end of track.

Joanna & Iain MacLeod
Homestead Farm,
Canon Frome, Ledbury HR8 2TG

Tel	01531 670268
Fax	01531 670210
Email	cloudie@tiscali.co.uk

Travel Club Offer. See page 290.

Entry 46   Map 2

North Court

The garden: North Court's astonishing 15 acres have developed over the last four centuries into a garden of historical interest and a paradise for plantsmen. The Isle of Wight remains warm well into the autumn, and in its downland-sheltered position the garden exploits its micro-climate to the full. Able to specialise in such exotics as bananas and echiums, the Harrisons have developed a sub-tropical garden; higher up the slope behind are Mediterranean terraces. There's extensive variety: the chalk stream surrounded with bog plants, the knot garden planted with herbs, the walled rose garden, the sunken garden, the one-acre kitchen garden, a Himalayan glade and a maritime area. All this represents a collection of 10,000 plants, some occasionally for sale – how do they do it? Modest John, the plantsman, says it is the good soil and atmosphere that allows everything to grow naturally and in profusion. But that is only half the story – he has left out the back-breakingly hard work and committment that have gone into it. They are knowledgeable too – he is a leading light in the Isle of Wight Gardens Trust, she was once the NGS county organiser for the island. Between them they have done a huge amount to encourage horticultural excellence in the area. *NGS, Good Gardens Guide, RHS, Isle of Wight Gardens Trust.*

The house: Think big and think Jacobean – built in 1615 by the then deputy governor of the Isle of Wight, North Court was once the manor house of a 2,000-acre estate. Extensively modified in the 18th century, the house has 80 rooms including a library housing a full-sized snooker table (yes, you may use it), and a 32-foot music room (you may play the piano, too). Bedrooms are large, in two separate wings, but although it all sounds terribly grand, this is a warm and informal family home – and your hosts more than likely to be found in gardening clothes. Autumn is an excellent and less busy time to visit.

Price	£65–£100. Singles £40–£50.
Rooms	6 twins/doubles.
Meals	Occasional light meals. Pub 3-minute walk through gardens.
Closed	Rarely.
Directions	From Newport, drive into Shorwell; down a steep hill, under a rustic bridge & right opposite thatched cottage. Signed.

John & Christine Harrison
North Court,
Shorwell PO30 3JG

Tel	01983 740415
Email	christine@northcourt.info
Web	www.northcourt.info

Hornbeams

The garden: Perfectly designed, brilliantly executed – Alison has come a long way since this garden was a field. She used to picnic here as a child, admire the view and dream about living here... The garden now surrounds the house and is bursting with plants. At the front are roses, camellias, lavender and acers in pots; a blackthorn and hawthorn hedge is grown through with golden hop, vines and more roses. By the front gate is a spring bed, then a purple bed leading to a white-scented border of winter flowering clematis and magnolias. An immaculate herb garden is spiked with tall fennel, the vegetable garden has raised beds and a morello cherry tree, and the orchard hums with fecundity. Winter and autumn beds are filled with interest and colour: snake-bark maple, dusky pink chrysanthemums, witch hazel and red-stemmed cornus. The herbaceous border is a triumph – colours move from pinks, purples and blues through apricots, creams and whites to the 'hot' end, and self-seeded intruders are swiftly dealt with. A little waterfall surrounded by lilies sits in the pond garden and rockery where hostas, ferns, astilbes, gunnera, bamboo and lilac compete for space. Rejoice in the knowledge that someone who has achieved their dream is so happy to share it with others. *RHS, Barham Horticultural Society.*

The house: Rolling hills and woodland, long views over luscious Kent, and a lovely garden that Alison has created entirely herself. This is a modern bungalow, a rare phenomenon in this book, a Scandia house brick-built from a Swedish kit. It is brilliant for wheelchair users and altogether easy and comfortable to be in, with floral-covered sofas and chairs and plain reproduction furniture. Alison, a beauty therapist and masseuse, is friendly and gracious. The house is so close to Dover that it is worth staying here for the night before embarking on the ferry fray.

Price	£75-£85. Singles £50.
Rooms	3: 1 double; 1 twin with separate bath/shower; 1 single with separate shower.
Meals	Occasional dinner. Pubs 1 mile.
Closed	Christmas.
Directions	From A2 Canterbury-Dover, towards Barham & Kingston. Right at bottom of hill by shelter, into The Street, Kingston to top of hill & right fork. 1st left on sharp right bend. Left into farm, keep right of barn.

Alison Crawley
Hornbeams, Jesses Hill,
Kingston, Canterbury CT4 6JD

Tel	01227 830119
Email	alison@hornbeams.co.uk
Web	www.hornbeams.co.uk

Woodmans

The garden: A leafy, colourful garden of about three quarters of an acre surrounded by paddocks. Sarah got the gardening bug from her parents, so when she found a garden that was already designed she felt confident about making a few changes. It feels rather Edwardian and old-fashioned, with long stretches of well-maintained lawn and a series of 'rooms' with large round shrub-filled beds — some winter-flowering and heavily scented. The whole garden is contained by mature trees and some pretty cross-hatch fencing forms a boundary between the garden and the fields beyond that open onto farmland. Colour is gentle: soft pink and cream tiles on the patio, faded wooden seats and tables, ancient lilac trees and the subtle blending of all that green. A stone bird bath sits on the lawn, there are some interesting stone statues, a raised pond with a small fountain tinkles away and there's a pretty rockery with wooden edges. The front garden faces north and is filled with things that thrive there, including hydrangeas. Roses and clematis tumble from many of the trees wafting their delicious scent in early summer, pots and hanging baskets are filled with flowers. Traditionalists will be happy here; it is amazingly peaceful.

The house: Not only are you in the depths of the countryside but you feel very private: your ground-floor bedroom is reached via a corner of the delightful garden with a seating area all your own. Step past greenery to the breakfast room, cosy with old pine table, dresser and flowers, for your bacon and eggs; if you don't feel like emerging, you may have breakfast brought to your room. This is a good stopover point for trips across the Channel — and you're a 15-minute drive from Canterbury and its glorious cathedral. *Babies welcome.*

Price	£70. Singles £35.
Rooms	1 double.
Meals	Dinner, 3 courses, £22.50. Packed lunch £6.50. Pub/restaurant 1 mile.
Closed	Rarely.
Directions	From A2, 2nd exit to Canterbury. Follow ring road & B2068 for Hythe. Over A2, through Lower Hardres, past Granville pub. Right to Waltham; 1.5 miles after Waltham, right into Hassell St; 4th on left.

Sarah Rainbird
Woodmans, Hassell Street,
Hastingleigh, Ashford TN25 5JE

Tel	01233 750250
Email	sarah.rainbird@googlemail.com

Travel Club Offer. See page 290.

Entry 49   Map 4

Bunkers Hill

The garden: From seats in different rooms in this treeful garden, you particularly notice the birdlife. There's a bird-feeding station that attracts many species, and busy flutterings in and out of mature trees and shrubs all over the garden. The terrace is planted with pots of lilies, roses and fuchsia, and from here the eye is drawn down between yew hedges and two pairs of swelling conifers to the little white dovecote at the end. Behind it, the layers of white blooms on the massive *Viburnum plicatum* 'Mariesii' are the spring focal point. Down between mixed borders and a tapestry beech hedge dividing the garden into two halves, round a mound of wisteria, or behind a thicket of hydrangeas, rhododendrons and hollies, sits another bench in a sunny clearing. Best of all: a gorgeous summer house at the far end, overlooking paddocks, ideal for sunset-watching. Scent rises from the border of shrub roses in this little secret garden: a 'Paul's Himalayan Musk' has dived up a silver birch, 'Wedding Day' has taken over an old prunus. Nicola took over her mother-in-law's garden when she moved here: rather than make drastic changes she has gently nurtured and gradually developed her inheritance, and the garden reflects her quiet affection for it.

The house: The garden room is an inspiration: not so much a conservatory, more a proper room, with windows all round and doors onto the terrace. Breakfasts are served here at a round table, in among the pots of jasmine and chrysanthemums. Nicola is a natural at looking after guests and garden, ducks and hens (delicious breakfast eggs), two dogs and cat called Spice – there's a relaxed and rural feel. The sitting room is low-beamed and oak-panelled, with a wood-burning stove. Play tennis, retreat to the summer house, step upstairs to a peaceful, pretty bedroom with a comfy bed and a lovely garden view.

Price	£80. Singles £55.
Rooms	1 twin with separate bath & shower.
Meals	Pubs/restaurants 4-5 miles.
Closed	November-February.
Directions	From M20 junc. 8, A20 east for Ashford. At Lenham, left to Warren St. On for 1 mile. Harrow pub on right. Bear left. After 300 yds, 3-way junc, sharp left. House 4th on left.

Nicola Harris
Bunkers Hill,
Lenham ME17 2EE

Tel   01622 858259

Entry 50   Map 4

Pope's Hall

The garden: Veronica and William came here in 1961 when the house and garden were almost derelict. Now these beautiful 2.5 acres are separated into three areas and, apart from a large oak and two yews, Veronica has planted everything herself, from seeds and cuttings grown in the greenhouse. The pond garden has a top pond with a small waterfall, while a sturdy cherub clutches a goose from whose mouth water cascades. Amble round the lower pond to admire the ornamental planting and fat water lilies while listening to the call ducks. Other touches of formality include the pot-lined drive bursting with agapanthus in summer, a courtyard with stone troughs and a variegated maple; from there, an archway of roses and honeysuckle leads to the main garden. Relax among smooth lawns, shrub areas, roses and trees, which in turn lead down to an elegant display of birch trees underplanted with snowdrops and dogwood. Hydrangeas do well, growing along the old wall that hides the swimming pool and beside a very large old Kentish barn. Rhododendrons and azaleas thrive, wildlife twitters and swoops, and two friendly terriers laze beneath the spreading horse chestnut tree next to a circle of box hedging. Come for more than one night and you can stay all day – bliss.

The house: Wind through the charming village to this listed house that dates from 1212, with a madly sloping roof, uneven floors and a riot of beams and timber inside. Step down into the salmon-pink dining room for a breakfast of local produce served at a solid oak table; William and Veronica are cheerful and welcoming. Old-fashioned bedrooms are a good size and deeply comfortable; bathrooms are spanking clean and sport thick towels, lovely soaps. This is a pleasant antidote to bling culture, so come to unwind – and it's only 40 minutes from the Channel tunnel. *Dogs welcome in outside heated kennel, £5 per night.*

Price	£70-£85. Singles from £50.
Rooms	3: 1 twin; 1 double, 1 twin sharing bath.
Meals	Pub 0.5 miles.
Closed	Rarely.
Directions	From M2, A249 towards Sittingbourne. 1st left at roundabout on A2; through Newington, 1st left to Hartlip.

William Wakeley
Pope's Hall, The Street,
Hartlip, Sittingbourne ME9 7TL

Tel	01795 842315
Fax	01795 841746
Email	william.wakeley@btinternet.com
Web	www.popeshall-bedandbreakfast.co.uk

Entry 51   Map 4

Wickham Lodge

The garden: Who would believe so much fecundity could be squeezed into one half acre? Cherith has known and loved this walled garden – 14 small gardens that flow into one – for over 40 years. Many plants were used in Tudor times (the business of identification is unfaltering), with Victorian cottage-garden plants being popped in over the years. Starting at the top end is the kitchen garden, a horn of plenty sprinkled with spring bulbs and cultivated wisely, 'companion planting' controlling pests and diseases. Then a fruit grove, a secret garden, a Cornish haven, a rose walk fragrant with over one hundred Old English shrub roses. In the Japanese garden, a stairway of railway sleepers topped with pebbles winds serenely up to a circular terrace enfolded by winter flowering shrubs. Later this transforms into a cool green oasis, while the most central section of the garden opens up to its summery palette of purples, pinks, whites and blues. Wander further… to the gravelled hop garden, where a rustic pergola supports hops from the river bank, and a topiary terrace (with goldfish pond) nudges the Tudor back of the house. To the front, a boatyard garden by the river – boats bob by at high tide, birds at low. The drive is edged with lavender and you park among vines. *NGS.*

The house: The onetime gatehouse to the big house on the hill looks Georgian, but started life Tudor: two lodges woven into one. Cherith has loved the place since she was a young woman. Be spoiled by traditional comforts, a riverside setting and a log-warmed drawing room with the greenest of views. The bedroom overlooking the river is fresh and airy with linen quilts on white metal beds; the Tudor Room is low-ceilinged with pretty pine and Victorian-style 'rain bath' (amazing). Have breakfast in the garden, lunch in Canterbury and supper in the village; its pubs, restaurants and 14th-century bridge ooze history and charm.

Price	£90. Singles £45–£55.
Rooms	3: 1 twin/double, 1 single; 1 double with separate bath.
Meals	Pubs/restaurants 100 yds.
Closed	Rarely.
Directions	From M20 junc. 5. Follow signs for Aylesford. Over crossing and bridge. At T- junc. left into village. Left 100 yds after traffic lights, directly after the Chequers Pub.

Richard & Cherith Bourne
Wickham Lodge, The Quay,
73 High Street, Aylesford ME20 7AY

Tel	01622 717267
Fax	01622 792855
Email	wickhamlodge@aol.com
Web	www.wickhamlodge.co.uk

Ethical Collection: Food.
See page 294 for details

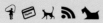

Rock Farm House

The garden: Plantsmen will be happy here. In the Seventies, when her children were young, Sue ran a nursery at Rock Farm that built up a considerable reputation. It closed in 2000, but her collection of interesting plants continues to be celebrated in her own garden. She knows from experience what plants grow best in these alkaline conditions, and they perform for her. The evergreen *Berberis stenophylla* provides a striking backdrop to the large herbaceous border – 90-foot long and, in places, 35-foot wide. Bulbs grown along the hedge are superceded by herbaceous plants; as these grow, the dying bulb foliage behind is neatly hidden from view. The oriental poppies in May herald the outburst of colour that lasts from June to September, and, to encourage wildlife, cutting down is delayed until January. The bog garden that lies below the house is filled with candelabra primulas, trollius, astilbes, day lilies, gunnera, lythrum, filipendulas and arum lilies: a continuous flowering from April to July. In a further area – around two natural ponds – contrasting conifer foliage interplanted with herbaceous perennials is set against a backdrop of Kentish woodland; superb groupings of hostas and ferns grow in shady areas. A delightful spot. *NGS, Good Gardens Guide, RHS Garden Finder.*

The house: This is a charming Kentish farmhouse, its beams fashioned from recycled ships' timbers from Chatham dockyard. Bedrooms are simple, traditional, lovely, one with a four-poster bed. Walls are pale or pure white, bedheads floral and furniture antique; the bedroom in the Victorian extension has a barrel ceiling and two big windows that look eastwards over the bog garden to the glorious Kentish Weald. Stairs lead down into the dining room with its lovely old log fire. Expect free-range eggs from the farm, homemade jams and local honey for breakfast.

Price	£75. Singles £50.
Rooms	3: 1 double, 1 twin; 1 twin with separate bath/shower.
Meals	Restaurant within 1 mile.
Closed	Christmas Day.
Directions	From Maidstone A26 to Tonbridge. At Wateringbury lights, left B2015. Right up Gibbs Hill; 1st right down drive, past converted oast house on right. Farm next.

Mrs Sue Corfe
Rock Farm House, Gibbs Hill,
Nettlestead, Maidstone ME18 5HT

Tel	01622 812244
Fax	01622 812244
Web	www.rockfarmhousebandb.co.uk

Boyton Court

The garden: A stunning series of slopes and terraces that swoop southwards with breathtaking views over the Weald to Tenterden and Sissinghurst. A natural spring feeds a series of four ponds packed around with primulas and other damp-loving plants; the top pond takes the Alhambra in Granada as a source, giving a Moorish feel. An octagonal pool with a fountain forms a striking centre piece surrounded by a very pretty parterre garden – designed on a paper tablecloth in New York when Richard was briefly stranded there after 9/11. Water flows down a stepped rill to the lower level: a rectangular pond full of fish and water lilies, an iris bed with *Verbena bonariensis* for late summer interest. The bottom, separate pond is wilder with a rowing boat, willows and *Betula jacquemontii*. Below the house is a bog garden with a mass of arum lilies, filipendula, eupatorium and other damp-loving varieties. Gaze over the blue and purple striped lavender bank from the terrace, enjoy a new border with drifts of grasses – especially interesting in late summer – and an exquisite rose garden with a selection of David Austin repeat-flowering roses underplanted with hardy geraniums. Perfection in two-and-a-half acres. *NGS.*

The house: Higgledy-piggledy but immaculate. A truly handsome listed house – 16th century brick-and-tile-hung, with Victorian additions. Richard and Patricia are helpful and friendly and have created a comfortable, elegant and relaxing home. There's a soft-blue drawing room with views over the garden and stacks of books. Aga breakfast is lovely; sausages with hops and other local produce. Soft colours in the bedrooms too – terracotta or apricot – with more views and pretty tiles in the bathrooms. You have privacy and your own kitchen if you choose the stable, and a terrace in the garden. *Minimum stay two nights at weekends.*

Price	£105. Singles £65.
Rooms	3: 1 double, 1 twin.
	Stable: 1 double/family.
Meals	Dinner, £25, by arrangement.
	Pubs 1 mile.
Closed	Christmas & New Year.
Directions	From M20, junc. 8, A20. Right at
	r'bout onto B2163, left onto A274.
	In S. Valence left at King's Head.
	Through village with chapel on right.
	After 0.5 miles right at 1st x-roads;
	house on left past barn.

Richard & Patricia Stileman
Boyton Court,
Sutton Valence ME17 3BY

Tel	01622 844065
Fax	01622 843913
Email	richstileman@aol.com

Entry 54 Map 4

The Ridges

The garden: The story of Barbara's garden starts in the 1970s when she used to help her mother with their garden centre. The more she learned, the more her interest grew: by the time her children had grown and flown she was hooked. Realising the potential of the garden, she began restoring and developing. The old apple trees lining the path were pruned, but not much else is recognisable now; instead, dense cottage garden planting demonstrates Barbara's eye for combinations of colour, form and foliage. Through a living arch, a lawned area is fringed with bright foliaged specimen trees cleverly positioned to shine against dark copper beech, holly and rhododendron. This shelter protects such tender plants as windmill palm and *Magnolia grandiflora*: a lovely setting for a Victorian-style glass house used for entertaining. In a natural looking stream garden damp-loving plants such as rodgersia and gunnera grow down towards a pool, while a 'Paul's Himalayan Musk' runs rampant over trellis and trees. An old buttressed wall has been uncovered to create a new, naturally planted quiet area, with scented plants and herbs to attract butterflies and bees. Let Barbara take you on a tour: the history is fascinating. *NGS, Good Gardens Guide.*

The house: John and Barbara look after you in a lovely old mill-owner's house built in the 1700s, in Barbara's family since 1951. Traditional bedrooms are upstairs with pale colours, flowery fabrics, patterned walls and wrought-iron beds; breakfast is downstairs in a cosy room overlooking the garden, with a log-burner for chilly mornings. Ornaments and pictures abound. The magnificent West Pennine Moors are great for walkers and cyclists – those who choose to brave the Commonwealth Games Course, or pootlers who can amble along the woods and reservoirs below the Pike. Both garden and welcome will delight you.

Price	From £70. Singles from £40.
Rooms	4: 2 doubles; 1 twin/double, 1 single sharing bath.
Meals	Pub within walking distance.
Closed	Christmas & New Year.
Directions	M6 junc. 27 or M61 junc. 8 for Chorley. Follow A6 ring road, taking mini r'bout for Cowling & Rivington. On down Cowling Brow, past Spinners Arms pub. House a few hundred yds further, on right.

John & Barbara Barlow
The Ridges, Weavers Brow,
Limbrick, Chorley PR6 9EB

Tel	01257 279981
Email	barbara@barlowridges.co.uk
Web	www.bedbreakfast-gardenvisits.com

Entry 55   Map 6

Baumber Park

The garden: If I were a bird I would go and live in this garden. Just over an acre of delicious smelling flowers, shrubs and hedges (sea buckthorn because the thrushes like the berries). "Scent is the thing," says Clare and even her favourite daffodil, 'Pheasants Eye', smells lovely. Follow a formal gravel front bordered by lonicera hedges, under a solid pergola over which golden hop and honeysuckle battle for the sky, to lawn and large borders full of sweet-smelling roses, eleagnus, buddleia, sedum and a maturing pocket handkerchief tree – planted to commemorate an anniversary! A box parterre is being created in the vegetable garden and beds are full, colourful and scented – thousands of bulbs pop up in the spring. There's a vast cherry tree underplanted with more bulbs, periwinkles and holly, a peony bed interplanted with sweet-smelling viburnum, and then a lovely whitebeam arch through which peeps a wildflower meadow. Few large trees have been planted so views are un-hindered and an old pond is planted around with native species only – for the wildlife, lucky things. A small quantity of interesting plants are for sale – propagated by Clare. *Trustee of Lincolnshire Wildlife Trust & manager of one of their nature reserves locally.*

The house: Lincoln red cows and Longwool sheep ruminate in the fields around this rosy-brick farmhouse – once a stud that bred a Derby winner. The old watering pond is now a haven for frogs, newts and toads; birds sing lustily. Maran hens conjure delicious eggs and Clare – a botanist – is hugely knowledgeable about the area. Bedrooms are light and traditional with mahogany furniture, and there is a heart-stopping view through an arched landing window. And a grass tennis court, a guest sitting room with log fire, and a dining room with local books. This is good walking, riding and cycling country, with quiet lanes. *Minimum stay two nights at weekends in high season.*

Price	£58–£62. Singles from £35.
Rooms	3: 2 doubles; 1 twin with separate bath.
Meals	Pubs/restaurants 4 miles.
Closed	Christmas & New Year.
Directions	From A158 in Baumber take road towards Wispington & Bardney. House 300 yds down on right.

Mike & Clare Harrison
Baumber Park,
Baumber, Horncastle LN9 5NE

Tel	01507 578235
Fax	01507 578417
Email	mail@baumberpark.com
Web	www.baumberpark.com

 Travel Club Offer. See page 290.

Kelling House

The garden: When Sue arrived in 1999 she kept only a few good shrubs and mature trees; the rest she bulldozed. Now French windows and doors lead directly onto the generous flagged terrace with its young box-edged parterre filled with herbs. Clumps of lavender, rosemary and sage give a mediterranean feel and scent the house but it is also a lovely place to sit and admire the rest – in particular, the wide bed of summer-flowering perennials: sweet-scented white phlox, elegant perovskia with its lavender blue spikes and grey foliage, and dramatic acanthus. From here the lawn runs to the southern boundary, while a curving herbaceous border softens the eastern boundary and leads to a small area of young ornamental trees. The western beds reveal tulip and walnut trees interspersed with shrubs and grasses. This is a young garden but it's charming and well planted with good lawns and unexpected surprises that invite inspection... there are interesting small trees and flowering shrubs that include grey-leafed cistus, santolina and rue. In summer, colours are pink, white and blue. Belvoir Castle is worth visiting – as are the magnificent cathedrals of Lincoln and Peterborough.

The house: Dating from 1785, three old cottages are now a long, low, rose-covered house of gentle rubble stone with a pantile roof, a pretty painted gate edged with lolling hollyhocks and a super garden. Well-proportioned rooms have good English furniture, well-made thick curtains and interesting paintings; the creamy sitting room overlooks the quiet street on one side and the garden on the other. Bedrooms are softly coloured with a pretty mix of checks, stripes and plain white cotton. Sue is delightful and looks after you without fuss, breakfast will set you up for the day.

Price	From £75. Singles from £45.
Rooms	3: 1 double; 1 double with separate bath, 1 single sharing bath (let to same party only).
Meals	Dinner £25, by arrangement. Packed lunch £7.50. Pub/restaurant 3-min. walk.
Closed	Rarely.
Directions	From A1, B1174 for Grantham; then A607 for Belton & Barkston. In Barkston, 2nd left on to West Street opp. village green and Stag pub. House on left opp. green cottage.

Ms Sue Evans
Kelling House, 17 West Street,
Barkston, Grantham NG32 2NL

Tel	01400 251440
Email	sue.evans7@btinternet.com
Web	www.kellinghouse.co.uk

38 Killieser Avenue

The garden: Winkle is a gardener to the last tip of her green fingers. She is devoted to gardening, garden design, and collecting plants: from modern grasses to old-fashioned cottage favourites. Hence this ravishing garden in Streatham's conservation area. The simple long rectangle of the garden's space has been magicked into three compartments, each with a character of its own, decorated with the finest plants: myriad lessons to be learned for town gardeners the moment they step into this south-facing plot. Certain items stand out: a lofty rose arch, a water feature, a carefully worked parterre and a dry gravel garden with drought-tolerant plants. Expect deep borders of whites, pinks and blues, obelisks festooned with clematis, topiary to give form, wonderful old roses – mostly courtesy of Peter Beales. A blacksmith forged the gothic garden seat where you sit surrounded by colour and scent, a blue wisteria adorns the back of the pretty Victorian house, old London bricks form patterns on the final terrace. Containers are stuffed with agapanthus and other beauties around the patio, a perfect place to relax. Winkle has won first prize in the English Garden best town garden award, and she organises small, private garden tours – Japanese visitors love her. *Assistant County Organiser for NGS, Good Gardens Guide.*

The house: The Haworths have brought country-house elegance – and the fruits of far-flung travels – to South London. Few people do things with as much natural good humour as Winkle, whose passions are cooking, gardening and garden history. The house glows, the attention to detail is striking, and you breakfast in a charming farmhouse kitchen. Bedrooms are spacious yet cosy: crisp duvets, lamb's wool rugs, fine fabrics, waffle robes, the scent of roses. All on a quiet residential street, and Streatham Hill station a three-minute walk; you can be in Victoria in 15 minutes. Fabulous food, too. *Children over 12 welcome.*

Price	£90-£95. Singles from £60.
Rooms	2: 1 twin; 1 single with separate bath.
Meals	Dinner £28.
Closed	Occasionally.
Directions	5-minute walk from Streatham Hill station (15 minutes to Victoria); 15-minute walk from Balham tube.

Winkle Haworth
38 Killieser Avenue, Streatham Hill,
London SW2 4NT

Tel	020 8671 4196
Fax	020 8761 4196
Email	winklehaworth@hotmail.com

Travel Club Offer. See page 290.

24 Fox Hill

The garden: The Haighs' home in the sweet seclusion of Fox Hill has a small gravelled front garden with bobbles of box and a standard holly – an eye-catching frontage for the pretty Victorian house – but there's much, much more to come. The long rectangular back garden has been completely re-designed and now bursts with colour and interest in every direction. Sue, who once worked at the Chelsea Physic Garden and is a true plant-lover, has cleared and re-planted paved areas by the house and built a raised pond for her beloved fish. The delicate water plants are guarded by tall, spiky agaves that thrust skywards from their containers. Climbers snake up walls, trellises and an arch, while water cascades soothingly from a waterfall into the pond. She has nurtured a few of the plants that were there when she arrived, a thriving ceanothus and a weeping pear tree among them, but otherwise started with a clean slate. To add a final flourish and to mark her pleasure at having her first-ever garden shed to play with, she has planted a 'Liquid Amber' sweet gum outside its door. This is a relatively young garden packed with promise.

The house: This part of London is full of sky, trees and wildlife; Pissarro captured on canvas the view up the hill in 1870 and the original painting can be seen in the National Gallery. There's good stuff everywhere – things hang off walls and peep over the tops of dressers; bedrooms are stunning, with antiques, textiles, paintings and big, firm beds. Sue, a graduate of Chelsea College of Art, puts guests at ease with intelligence and humour and has created a very special garden, too. She will cook supper (sea bass, maybe, stuffed with herbs); Tim often helps with breakfasts.

Price	£90–£100. Singles £50.
Rooms	3: 1 twin/double; 1 double, 1 twin sharing shower.
Meals	Dinner £30–£35. Pubs/restaurants 5-minute walk.
Closed	Rarely.
Directions	Train: Crystal Palace (7-min. walk). Collection possible. Good buses to West End & Westminster.

Sue & Tim Haigh
24 Fox Hill, Crystal Palace,
London SE19 2XE

Tel	020 8768 0059
Email	suehaigh@hotmail.co.uk
Web	www.foxhill-bandb.co.uk

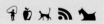 Travel Club Offer. See page 290.

Entry 59   Map 3

Manor House Farm

The garden: A huge labour of love. Libby and Robin have been passionately working on this very special garden since 1965 when it was meadowland and some old cattle yards. Now it is a peaceful, seemingly effortless oasis with approximately 12 'compartments' over four acres, planted impeccably so that year-round interest is maintained. In the Taj garden, a neat conservatory is filled with vines and plumbago and overlooks the splendid pond... there are some delightful places to sit here, surrounded by shrubs. It is resplendent with tulips in spring and scented roses in summer. Behind the house is a smooth lawn with more roses, shrubs and an old yew tree by the churchyard wall; the other trees have been planted by Robin – mimosa, eucalyptus and a small arboretum. Wander through a rose tunnel from here into yet another area, then down a pleached lime avenue to a woodland area carpeted in snowdrops in winter. Vegetables are grown for the table, but also soft fruit – masses of it – and their own asparagus; a flock of 50 chickens provides the breakfast eggs. Wildlife is abundant with barn owls, rabbits and both sika and muntjac deer. Robin and Libby (she the brain, he the muscle) confess that they can spend ten hours a day in the garden – not always agreeing on plans!

The house: In the private stable wing and next-door cottage of this traditional Norfolk farmhouse, surrounded by four acres of lovingly tended gardens, are beautiful fresh rooms with wildly comfortable beds and a sitting room for guests; expect antiques, colourful rugs and fresh flowers. Breakfast, served in the elegant dining room of the main house, is home-grown and delicious: fruit, eggs from the Welsummer hens, and bacon and sausages from their own happy pigs. Libby and Robin have won conservation awards for the farm – and the glorious North Norfolk coast is 20 minutes away. *Smoking allowed in parts of the house.*

Price	£90–£100. Singles £50–£65.
Rooms	2: 1 double, 1 twin/double.
Meals	Restaurant 1.5 miles.
Closed	Rarely.
Directions	A1065 Swaffham-Fakenham road. 6 miles on, through Weasenham. After 1 mile, right for Wellingham. House on left, next to church.

Elisabeth Ellis
Manor House Farm, Wellingham,
Fakenham, King's Lynn PE32 2TH

Tel	01328 838227
Fax	01328 838348
Email	libby.ellis@btconnect.com
Web	www.manor-house-farm.co.uk

 Travel Club Offer. See page 290.

Entry 60   Map 7

Litcham Hall

The garden: This superb garden has given the family a lot of pleasure over the 40 years since they came to Litcham Hall. The swimming pool has provided fun for children and visitors, but John and Hermione have found the design and planting of their garden from scratch the most satisfying project. Yew hedges make a dramatic backdrop for herbaceous borders and the framework for a sunken area with a little lily pond and fountain. Strolling along mown paths through their wild garden is a delight in spring when the snowdrops, azaleas and bluebells are out: in summer you emerge from this spinney through a pergola covered in climbing roses. Behind the house the swimming pool is sheltered in part of a double-walled garden, with a brick-arched veranda loggia down one side – a wonderful spot for relaxing in mediterranean weather. The walled Italian garden was inspired by the desire to put to best use some beautiful inherited stone urns. Now artfully positioned in a parterre of lavender-filled, box-edged beds, the urns make an elegant finishing touch to a formal composition entirely suited to the period of the house. *Open occasionally for the Red Cross & NGS.*

The house: For the whole of the 19th century this was Litcham's doctor's house and today, over 200 years after it was built, the red-brick Hall remains at the centre of the community. This is a thoroughly English home with elegant proportions; the hall, drawing room and dining room are gracious and beautifully furnished. The big-windowed guest rooms look onto the stunning garden where you are free to wander. Household hens lay the breakfast eggs, and the garden provides soft fruit for the table in season. John and Hermione are friendly and charming. *Children, dogs & use of pool by arrangement.*

Price	£70-£90. Singles by arrangement.
Rooms	3: 1 double, 1 twin; 1 twin with separate bath.
Meals	Occasional dinner, £25. Pub/restaurant 3 miles.
Closed	Christmas.
Directions	From Swaffham, A1065 north for 5 miles, then right to Litcham on B1145. House on left on entering village. Georgian red-brick with stone balls on gatepost.

John & Hermione Birkbeck
Litcham Hall,
Litcham, King's Lynn PE32 2QQ

Tel	01328 701389
Fax	01328 701164
Email	hermionebirkbeck@hotmail.com

Entry 61   Map 7

Mill Common House

The garden: John and Wendy have always treated their guests like friends; their walled garden receives a similar level of tender loving care. This gently sloping garden is protected from the salty north-east wind by a thick 30-foot-high conifer hedge, which allows a wide variety of flowering shrubs to flourish — hydrangeas do beautifully here — interspersed with Wendy's favourite annuals such as *Nicotiana silvestris* and *Verbena bonariensis*. Roses scramble through trees, over walls, and up the extensive 200-year-old brick and flint barns. Gentle 'New Dawn' frames the front door. To the front of the house the old farm pond is surrounded by grasses, camassias, phormiums and valerian; to the rear is an established *Viburnum tinus* hedge surrounding the New Garden, where stunning south-facing 'hot' borders provide colour from early summer to the frosts. In the large Victorian-style conservatory, plumbago and geraniums weave their way through the wall trellis, while the many geraniums and orchids add colour to the sills. Wendy is a talented flower arranger and loves to grow herbs, lavender, agapanthus and lilies in artistically arranged pots around the terrace. *RHS, NT, The Norwich Cathedral Flower Guild, Norfolk Gardens Trust.*

The house: In undiscovered Norfolk, an elegant Georgian conversion of an older cottage. Gorgeous chintzes throughout, and exceptionally comfortable bedrooms with toile de Jouy patchwork bedspreads and heaps of cushions. Bathrooms are lovely too, with easy chairs and Norfolk Lavender soaps; one overlooks the walled garden and has a charming roll top bath. Wendy's Aga-cooked breakfasts in the conservatory are a treat. Flowers everywhere, log fires, French windows that lead onto the terrace: such a cosseting place to stay. And plenty of inspirational gardens and historic houses and churches nearby.

Price	From £72. Singles £46.
Rooms	2: 1 twin/double; 1 double with separate bath.
Meals	Pubs/restaurants 5 miles.
Closed	Christmas.
Directions	A1151 from Norwich through Wroxham. Left to Walcott. At T-junc. left for Walcott. After 3.5 miles, opposite Lighthouse Inn on right. Left, on unmarked road, 1 mile to the Y-junc.; house on left at next Y-junc.

Mrs Wendy Pugh
Mill Common House, Ridlington,
North Walsham NR28 9TY

Tel	01692 650792
Email	johnpugh@millcommon.freeserve.co.uk
Web	www.millcommonhouse.co.uk

Entry 62   Map 7

Sallowfield Cottage

The garden: A deceptive one acre, but the beautiful large pond in front of the house acts as a huge mirror and reflects tall trees, island beds and the building itself, giving a Norwegian 'lake impression' of space and green. When Caroline arrived it was swamped and overgrown; she only left what she decided was interesting. This included an impressive swamp cypress, a weeping ash, lots of viburnums, magnolias, a chimonanthus and an as yet unidentified acer she calls the "firework tree" because of its fiery autumn colour. There are also some very old trees: an enormous willow and a vast ash. Caroline has a real knack for positioning plants – they all thrive where they're placed and look good together; lilacs and pinks, shades of green and the odd splash of dark red or yellow against the perfect backdrop. An old ditch has been turned into a sunken path with a trimmed hedge on one side and a herbaceous bank on the other. Clematis and honeysuckle wind through trees and shrubs and all the shapes and colours are soft – there's no ugly rigidity. A tiny, enclosed courtyard has been constructed against one wall of the house and a pink *Clematis texensis* shoots up it; another wall is capped by curly tiles and there are pots filled with hostas. The pale terracotta-floored conservatory is prettily canopied with vine leaves.

The house: Caroline's cottage is so crammed with family treasures, it takes time to absorb the splendour: in the drawing room, gorgeous prints and paintings, books, unusual furniture and decorative lamps. One (not huge but handsome) bedroom has a Regency-style canopied bed and decoration to suit the house (1850); the attic room is large and lovely but there are steep stairs. The garden is fascinating, with hedged rooms and a jungly pond that slinks between the trees. Caroline – and her pets – love having guests and if you have friends living locally she is happy to do lunch or dinner for up to 10. *Children over nine welcome.*

Price	£60. Singles £35.
Rooms	3: 1 double; 1 double with separate bath; 1 single with separate shower.
Meals	Lunch £10. Dinner from £20. Pub 2 miles.
Closed	Christmas & New Year.
Directions	A11 Attleborough-Wymondham. Take Spooner Row sign. Over x-roads beside Three Boars pub. 1 mile; left at T-junc. to Wymondham for 1 mile. Look for rusty barrel on left, turn into farm track.

Caroline Musker
Sallowfield Cottage, Wattlefield,
Wymondham NR18 9NX

Tel	01953 605086
Email	caroline.musker@tesco.net
Web	www.sallowfieldcottage.co.uk

Bressingham Hall

The garden: In 1953 Alan Bloom, founder of the legendary nursery and Dell Garden, wanted to experiment with new ways of growing hardy perennials in island beds. He first planted in front of the family home and as soon as he realised they were successful he planted in nearby meadows, eventually accumulating 48 beds covering six acres. By 1962 he had collected 5,000 species and varieties. His son Adrian joined the business in 1962 and became keen to do his own thing, initially using mainly conifers and heathers in Foggy Bottom Garden. Over the years Foggy Bottom has developed as a spectacular garden of year-round interest. The whole family have a passion for plants and the growth continues with The Summer Garden which holds the National Collection of Miscanthus. Adrian's Wood is bulging with North American origin plants, the Winter Garden is spectacular with its colourful cornus, snowdrops, early bulbs and hellebores, and the Fragrant Garden is packed with scented plants. It is a privilege to stay here, in the midst of these world-renowned gardens – and, of course, you can buy plants and take them home with you. Whether you have a large plot, a tiny patch or just pots to fill there is inspiration for all.

The house: Past the famous steam museum and onto the mansion house, built in 1780 for the Squire of Bressingham. It's a handsome house with high ceilings, light-filled rooms and large sash windows with sensational garden views. All is deeply old-fashioned but that is part of the charm. You breakfast in a sunny, east-facing room on Grandad's rhubarb baked with brown sugar, locally cured bacon and local farm eggs. There's a sitting room with an open log fire and views, bedrooms are large and filled with books, magazines and easy chairs, bathrooms are clean and adequate, and Ian is delightful. *Minimum stay two nights at weekends.*

Price	£80. Singles £55. Entry to gardens & steam museum included.
Rooms	3: 1 double, 1 twin, 1 family room.
Meals	Pub/restaurant 0.25 miles.
Closed	November-March.
Directions	On the south side of the A1066, 2.5 miles west of Diss. Driveway 200 yds west of Garden Centre entrance.

Ian Tilden
Bressingham Hall,
Bressingham, Diss IP22 2AA

Tel	01379 687243
Email	b&b@bressinghamgardens.com
Web	www.bressinghamgardens.com

Westfield

The garden: When Colin and Vicky arrived here 35 years ago, the half-acre garden was a random forest of native trees. Drastic culling helped to give much-needed structure: they left a few indigenous trees and planted ornamental species (Indian bean tree, liquidambar, Ponderosa pine, black walnut). Then they set about creating three separate areas. The result is a meandering, engaging garden, completely surrounded by high walls or impenetrable hedge, which is stunning in spring, summer and autumn. Shrubs – philadelphus, weigelia, deutzia – mass together and deep borders glow with rare French irises, day lilies, penstemon or superb hellebores. The collection of unusual plants is growing all the time. Beside the new extension is a terrace which drops away to three walled areas with more beds and a weeping pear tree. Emma, Vicky's mother, came to live with them a couple of years ago and is obviously a presiding genius. Her pride and joy is the Victorian greenhouse, where she cherishes rare scented geraniums, jasmines and orchids. She is quite capable of putting in six hours gardening during the day before retiring to write her book on Chaucer. Two dogs and two cats keep a proprietorial eye and the birds are truly prolific.

The house: The surprises come thick and fast. First, after a rather unexceptional approach, the charm of the village. Then, behind a modern entrance, a rambling period house which was once two cottages. One, 18th-century and stone, has flagstone floors and its original pump; the other, Victorian and brick, has been joined to an outbuilding by an atrium-style extension so that its kitchen and living area seem almost part of the garden. Bedrooms are traditional, comfortable and have tea trays with bone china. You are welcomed by wonderful, down-to-earth people – this is a delightful place to stay.

Price	£60. Singles £35.
Rooms	2 twins/doubles sharing bathroom.
Meals	Pubs/restaurants within 3-15 minute walk.
Closed	Christmas, Boxing Day & New Year.
Directions	Proceed East from M1 junction 18 to Crick (aim at church spire). Park near church; walk back to main road, then down hill 100 yds to house.

Dr & Mrs C B Mynott
Westfield, 36 Main Road,
Crick, Northampton NN6 7TX

Tel   01788 822313
Email   cbm@mynott.com

Travel Club Offer. See page 290.

Ashdene

The garden: An imaginative, really special garden — with a huge 60-year-old paulownia which, excitingly, flowered recently. Both David and Glenys have done the hard work: a gravel and boulder garden tucked around the front of the house has scented plants for spring and autumn, two huge yews have been cut to tall stumps, then their later sproutings coaxed and designed by David — one into a spiral, the other into a witty Rastafarian topknot. There's a white spring garden and a woodland walk along serpentine brick paths with precisely coppiced hazels. A long grass walk up a slope takes you away from the house and is edged with hornbeam — rest at the top, a favourite quiet spot. There are over 50 species of damask roses, paths through brick-raised beds of mixed planting and a central circle of five pillars around an Ali Baba urn. Trellises of scented roses create hidden corners and add height. The vegetable garden is fecund but neat, the sunken garden and the terrace by the house have good seating areas. David's topiary is artistic and striking, including using an unusual muehlenbeckia; he's nicked a juniper into a table (his Chinese libation cup) and is training ivy along a tunnel of wire — so this is what retired surgeons do! Their use of chemical help with all this? None. An organic garden which attracts many birds (38 nests at the last count) and a centuries-old colony of bees. *NGS, RHS. Open for garden clubs & charities.*

The house: A mile west of bustling Southwell and its lovely Minster, this stunning rosy-bricked house was once the old manor house of Halam and dates from 1520. Much travelled, David and Glenys have packed their big, friendly, family house with wonderful paintings, samplers, embroidery, books on history and travel, lovely old rugs and comfortable furniture. Guests have their own drawing room with open fire and the bedrooms are gorgeous: pretty white bed linen, spotless bathrooms with fluffy towels and relaxing, neutral colours. Don't creep around on egg shells, come and go as you like — but do ask about the area, they know it well.

Price	£70. Singles £50.
Rooms	4: 2 doubles, 1 twin, 1 single.
Meals	Pub 4-minute walk.
Closed	Occasionally.
Directions	A1, then A617/A612 to Southwell. Take sign to Farnsfield. In Halam left at crossroads, past church, house 200 yds on left.

David Herbert
Ashdene, Halam,
Southwell NG22 8AH

Tel   01636 812335
Email   david@herbert.newsurf.net

Ethical Collection: Community; Food.
See page 294.

Entry 66   Map 6

Hernes

The garden: In 1968 Gillian and Richard took over the family estate with two full-time gardeners to look after the huge Victorian garden. When one of them died unexpectedly the then somewhat unhorticultural Gillian, with three children under four, knew something had to change. More than 40 years on the garden is mercifully a little smaller but it is in extremely capable hands. Some elements of the original Victorian layout remain: the wisteria arbour, the nut walk, the croquet lawn and the wild garden — Gillian's favourite spot. The garden has many family associations and memories: majestic Wellingtonias that mark the 21st birthdays of elder sons, the holly 'house' and the giant toadstool on which children love to perch like pixies, the ha-ha looking out to the old cricket meadow, the carpets of bulbs under the trees. New since the 1960s are the pool garden, the rose arbour (planted to celebrate Gillian's retirement as a school governor) and the hornbeam walk. The vegetable garden continues to supply delicious produce, and while Gillian plans new projects for the future (ask her about her philosophical "labyrinth of life"), she remains realistic about all that maintenance. This garden is essentially a gentle place for peaceful contemplation.

The house: Ramble through the ages in Hernes, home to five generations of the family. A stately but comfortable place to stay: a panelled hall with open fire and grand piano, a drawing room with original inglenook fireplace, a billiard room with easy chairs by a log stove. Large bedrooms overlook the garden; one has a fine four-poster, another a large sleigh bed. Long soaks in the Victorian blue claw-foot bath are a treat. On Sundays tuck into the traditional Ovey breakfast of porridge (in winter), kedgeree and boiled eggs — served in the dining room hung with family portraits.

Price	From £97.50. Singles from £67.50. Single-night bank holiday surcharge.
Rooms	3: 1 twin/double, 1 four-poster; 1 double with separate bath.
Meals	Pub/restaurants 1 mile.
Closed	December to mid-January & occasionally.
Directions	Over lights in centre of Henley as far as Town Hall. Left through car park; right onto Greys Rd for 2 miles; 300 yds after 30mph zone, 2nd drive on right; signed drive to main house.

Richard & Gillian Ovey
Hernes,
Henley-on-Thames RG9 4NT

Tel	01491 573245
Fax	01491 574646
Email	governor@herneshenley.com
Web	www.herneshenley.com

 Travel Club Offer. See page 290.

Entry 67   Map 3

Lakeside Town Farm

The garden: Theresa started taking gardening seriously years ago, when she and Jim moved into their home on their Oxfordshire farm. It all began with a rockery and is now a maturing multi-dimensional plant paradise. What was once sheep pasture is now one and a half acres of superbly planted, well-designed areas that range from the formal to the wonderfully wild. Theresa has created rockeries, scree beds and dramatic borders as well as a restful waterfall and two lakes. The garden, featured in *Ideal Home* last year, is divided into a series of well-defined areas, each with a mood of its own and with witty decorations including an old telephone kiosk and street lamp. You'll find a rose-smothered pergola, an ornamental grass border, specimen trees, manicured lawns and a glorious vegetable garden. Theresa is a self-confessed plantaholic and avidly collects new treasures – no wonder the garden has also been featured in the *Sunday Telegraph* and on *Gardener's World*! 'Albertine' roses wind through apple trees, a vigorous 'American Pillar' decorates an arch. Best of all is Theresa's supreme wildflower garden surrounding one of the ponds: a snowy mass of ox-eye daisies studded with corn cockle, corn marigolds and other wild beauties. A gem. *RHS*.

The house: A dream setting – and a picture-perfect farmhouse, built along traditional lines beside the lakes. The guest drawing room is large and light with sofas and chairs and a door to the garden for sunny evenings. Bedrooms have garden views, Victorian brass beds, pretty cushions and fresh flowers; there's even a little decanter of sherry and a fridge outside for your own bottles of wine. Wake up to the smell of freshly baked bread, and fill up on Jim's hearty breakfast. Independence lovers will adore the new garden lodge, shabby chic and romantic with your own little kitchen and veranda. *Minimum stay two nights.*

Price	From £75. Singles from £60.
Rooms	3: 1 twin; 1 double.
	Garden lodge: 1 double.
Meals	Pubs/restaurants 600 yds.
Closed	Rarely.
Directions	M40 junc. 6, B4009 for Princes Risborough; 2 miles, then 1st left in Kingston Blount for 300 yds, right into Brook Street, then immediately left down drive to last house, through automatic-opening wooden gates.

Ethical Collection: Food.
See page 294.

Cherry Tree pub.

Theresa & Jim Clark
Lakeside Town Farm, Brook Street,
Kingston Blount OX39 4RZ

Tel	01844 352152
Fax	01844 352152
Email	theresa@townfarmcottage.co.uk
Web	www.townfarmcottage.co.uk

Entry 68   Map 3

South Newington House

The garden: Arrive down the drive in June and you are engulfed by colour and scent – and roses wafting in that gentle, English-garden way. The Ainleys are a great team, work well together as organisers for the National Gardens Scheme, and have created two very special acres of garden in five acres of paddocks and grounds. A walled garden (its gate leading to a field of sheep) is surrounded by honeyed Hornton stone – an idyllic backdrop for roses and wisteria, and a parterre created with box topiary. The themed borders on the other side of the house are profusely and subtly planted. Hellebores, winter-flowering honeysuckle and cornus brighten winter days and the orchard is carpeted with snowdrops; daffodils and primroses welcome the spring. By summer the pond is a riot of water lilies and damselflies; misty autumn mornings shimmer with colour. The conservatory is filled with fragrant hoya, plumbago, stephanotis and jasmine: a perfect place to sit and view the garden. The huge kitchen garden provides a range of organic vegetables and soft fruit – asparagus and artichokes among other delights. Roberta's "gardeners" are her bantams: eggs don't come fresher or more free-range. *NGS, RHS.*

The house: Roberta and John are generous hosts and great fun. Their charming, listed, 17th-century hall house with flagged hall and oak staircase has three pretty bedrooms, some with mullioned windows and seats overlooking the gardens – immaculate retreats with crisp cotton on good beds and fresh flower arrangements. The converted farm building with its private, tiny sitting room and bedroom overlooks the walled garden and farm yard. In summer enjoy breakfast on the terrace: eggs from the hens, honey from the bees, local Gloucester Old Spot sausages and bacon, homemade bread and jams. *Discounts for three or more nights. Minium stay two nights.*

Price	£80. Singles £50.
Rooms	4: 2 doubles, 1 twin, all with separate bath. Cottage: 1 double.
Meals	Pubs/restaurants within 1.5 miles.
Closed	Rarely.
Directions	A361 Banbury to Chipping Norton. In South Newington 3rd left signed 'The Barfords'. 1st left down tree-lined drive.

Roberta & John Ainley
South Newington House,
South Newington, Banbury OX15 4JW

Tel	01295 721207
Email	rojoainley@btinternet.com
Web	www.southnewingtonhouse.co.uk

Ethical Collection: Environment; Food.
See page 294.

The Wilderness

The garden: Peter's grandfather was a great collector of seeds and cuttings from all over the world which encouraged his enthusiasm for growing things. Eight years ago the garden was re-designed by Peter and Tarn; they have added walkways and pergolas to link the different rooms, then planted new beds and – Tarn's great love – old-fashioned roses. They have achieved what they wanted, a garden that looks natural, stylish and maturing very nicely. A huge bouncy lawn leads to long pergola walkways with borders in front and behind, all smothered in roses, and a shrubbery with mounds of hebe, mahonia and climbing hydrangea. The croquet lawn looks out to an SSSI (with some rare wild orchids) and is bounded by a mixed beech and copper beech hedge, walnut and horse chestnut trees, a colourful shrub bed and a woodland bed with roses under a line of sycamores. An old espaliered pear climbs up the side of the house and there is a peaceful orchard, guarded by larger trees and an ancient folly. Bounded on one whole side by an ancient yew hedge the garden is protected and a haven for birds: pheasant, partridge and woodpeckers which potter and swoop alongside the smaller species. Geoff Hamilton's amazing Barnsdale garden is close by: a 'theme park' for gardeners.

The house: The Wilderness awaits you in a quietly elegant way. The pretty, secluded stone house dates from 1690 (although with some Georgian tampering) and is in a quiet village close to Rutland Water. The entrance hall is stone-flagged, the pale blue drawing room is large and inviting with books and games, you breakfast in the grand dining room with its high ceiling and huge windows. You're spoiled in the bedrooms – one pink and flouncy with Colefax & Fowler fabrics, the other bright lemon – and the separate bathrooms, with their power showers, unusual wallpapers and fluffy robes. Tarn is glamorous and fun, Peter is charming.

Price	£98.
Rooms	2: 1 twin/double with separate bath, 1 twin/double with separate shower.
Meals	Pub in village or within 5 miles.
Closed	Christmas & New Year.
Directions	From A1 to Empingham, once into village 250 yds past 30mph sign, right on Main Street. House on right behind stone wall with yew hedge - 50 Main Street - opposite School Lane.

Peter & Tarn Dearden
The Wilderness,
Empingham, Oakham LE15 8PS

Tel	01780 460180
Fax	01780 460121
Email	tarn@dearden-wilderness.co.uk
Web	www.rutnet.co.uk/wilderness

Yew Tree House

The garden: A well-established garden — about one-and-a-half acres — of lawns, woodland, shrubbery, flower beds, pond and wildlife area, linked by lots of grassed paths. From your terrace you can walk past the herb garden; backed by a fence made of coloured poles, with sculptural spirals dotted through its beds, this is a quirky delight. Round the house you then come to a terrace with tables and chairs leading onto smooth lawns enclosed by trees, some rare (a tulip tree, a weeping ash), and deep beds packed with colour. There's a serene pond, a homemade Stonehenge, an orchard brimming with apple trees, living willow structures, a secluded arbour and an arch into a very special circle of grass surrounded by shrubs and with a flower bed at its centre. Everything within the circle is painted blue: the sculpture, the rose pyramids and the bench. There are two woodland areas, one in the main garden underplanted with spring bulbs and shade-tolerant perennials, the other recently planted as native Shropshire broadleaf woodland. The peace is broken only by birdsong and there are plenty of places to sit and ponder, but you are not alone; Clive's sculptures — some up to 15 feet tall — lurk round corners and peek from bushes. Lovely.

The house: A dreamy rurality here in this much untrumpeted county, where the Montgomery canal makes its lazy way to Frankton Locks. One of Clive's huge sculptures greets you as you drive in to your neat, self-contained room with outside seating area. These are contemporary, almost hotel-like spaces, with matching furniture of a highly functional modern design. Art peppers the walls, floors are bamboo with modern rugs, beds have hugely comfortable toppers; bathrooms are small and bang up to date. You eat well: breakfast on local dry-cure bacon or 'savoury duck' (contains no duck!). Clive and Jo are warm, easy-going souls.

Price	£75–£85. Singles £55–£65.
Rooms	2: 1 double, 1 twin.
Meals	Dinner, 2-3 courses, £15–£18. Packed lunch £5–£6. Pubs 2-4 miles.
Closed	Never.
Directions	From Oswestry take A495 Whitchurch, 2.5 miles past Whittington enter Welsh Frankton; immediately before church turn right signed Lower Frankton. House 1.5 miles on right.

Clive & Jo Wilson
Yew Tree House, Lower Frankton,
Oswestry SY11 4PB

Tel	01691 622126
Email	info@yewtreebandb.co.uk
Web	www.yewtreebandb.co.uk

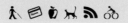

Lawley House

The garden: More than 50 types of rose bloom in wild profusion – including a 'Paul's Himalayan Musk' that vigourously scrambles through an acacia. Deep herbaceous borders glow with colour and the secret pond garden sparkles with water lilies. This was a weed-choked three acres of sloping ground when Jim and Jackie came on the scene, longer ago than they care to remember! Since then they have gardened devotedly and imaginatively, creating a richly planted design of lawns, beds, trees and shrubs to draw the eye across the valley to the hill scenery beyond. They began with a massive clearance programme which unearthed stone steps and the now restored pond. Today the mood is sunny, delightfully informal and traditional – they love scent and have carefully planted for year-round interest among different sections divided by immaculately tended lawns – badgers and moles permitting! Acid-loving plants such as rhododendrons and camellias thrive, so do the traditional garden flowers: lupins, sweet peas and delphiniums. A lovely country-house garden with long views – the Wrekin, Lawley and Caradoc hills are a glory and you can even spot distant Clee Hill on a clear day.

The house: Built on the lower slopes of north Long Mynd to take in the view, this imposing Victorian house is large and comfortable. You can lie in bed in the morning with the sunlight streaming in and gaze over exquisite countryside – or enjoy it all from the classical conservatory downstairs. William Morris fabrics and big furniture give a traditional feel; the baby grand that plays for you at breakfast (on request!) adds a humorous touch. Bedrooms are very comfortable with flowers, books, duckdown pillows, mini fridges; horse-racing enthusiasts Jackie and Jim are delightful and fun hosts.

Price	£50–£70. Singles £40–£55.
Rooms	3: 2 doubles, 1 twin/double.
Meals	Pub/restaurant 1.5 miles.
Closed	Christmas & New Year.
Directions	From Shrewsbury, south on A49. Ignore turn in Dorrington, keep on for 3 miles. 0.5 miles before Leebotwood, right to Smethcott. Follow signs uphill for 2 miles; drive on left just before Smethcott.

Jackie & Jim Scarratt
Lawley House, Smethcott,
Church Stretton SY6 6NX
Tel   01694 751236
Email   jscarratt@onetel.com
Web   www.lawleyhouse.co.uk

Travel Club Offer. See page 290.

Acton Pigot

The garden: Ferocious fecundity – as if the entire two-acre garden had been magically manured and then left to marinade. John's mother is a great gardener (if you want another treat ask to see her next-door paradise) and she laid out the structure. John and Hildegard have worked hard to bring it into line and the results are magnificent. Dividing the garden into sections the drive up to the house is heaving with huge euphorbias in raised aubretia-clad stone beds, there are thousands of bulbs, an iris bed, large shrubs planted through with ramblers and lovely giant yew balls for structure. The front garden is enclosed with a lawn (croquet in summer) and a huge late-flowering magnolia leans against the almost green house; the back section is all mixed borders with a walled garden by an old swimming pool where sun-lovers are planted. A vegetable, fruit and herb garden provides goodies for the kitchen. There are many rare shrubs and trees, and a wood for each of their three children. Scent is important, especially near the terrace – a wonderful spot for alfresco meals or simply sitting. The garden gently peters out with no boundary to open fields and a lake where ducks, geese, curlews and other water birds flap happily – go quietly and you will hear that lark rising. Hildegard says "you can't force nature" but she has done a jolly good persuading job.

The house: From the double room, with hand-printed wallpaper and oak chests, you look to Acton Burnell hill – England's first parliament was held here. The yellow room has lovely views of a lake, the garden and the Welsh hills; sunsets can be spectacular. Wooden doors, floors, carved settle and chests sit well with elegant furniture, fine prints and photographs. Happy in their role of hosts, the Owens spoil you with afternoon tea before a log fire, and their suppers are delicious. Parts of the house were built in 1660; the site is mentioned in the Domesday book. A restorative place run by lovely people.

Price	From £75. Singles £50.
Rooms	3: 1 double, 1 twin/double, 1 family room.
Meals	Pub 3 miles.
Closed	Christmas.
Directions	From A5 & Shrewsbury, onto A458 for Bridgnorth; 200 yds on, right to Acton Burnell. Entering Acton Burnell, left to Kenley; 0.5 miles, left to Acton Pigot; house 1st on left.

John & Hildegard Owen
Acton Pigot, Acton Burnell,
Shrewsbury SY5 7PH

Tel	01694 731209
Email	actonpigot@farming.co.uk
Web	www.actonpigot.co.uk

Entry 73 Map 6

The Croft Cottage

The garden: The Colly Brook bisects the property, tumbling some 350 yards through the south-facing garden created over ten years by Elizabeth and David – very special. Five bridges now connect the parts of the garden to one another; to the west is a vegetable patch, some herbaceous borders, a willow tunnel and a hazel coppice; to the east are the cottage, more borders, the orchard, the reflective garden and a duck house for the Indian runner ducks who keep the slugs at bay. Further upstream is the goose field with bee hives, geese, chickens and a wildflower meadow which bursts with orchids in June. Beyond this is the wood where there is an observation hide for watching the badgers: a rare treat! A wetland meadow has a pond which is home to moorhens, minnows and dragonflies; hundreds of hedging trees have been planted to create a windbreak. Because Elizabeth keeps bees, most of the plants are old cottage-type nectar or pollen producers; colour-themed beds include one devoted to hot yellows, reds and purples, another to blues, pinks and whites. You are welcome to stay all day in this paradise if you like – have a picnic just outside your room, then badger-watch in the evening. It is a gorgeous, peaceful spot.

The house: Drop from the heights of Clee Hill down narrowing lanes and a secluded valley to find this old estate worker's cottage beside a stream; its new extension is where you will stay with complete independence. The Hatchells treat you to eggs from the ducks and hens, lovely homemade marmalade and honey from the bees; enjoy it all while watching the ducks through the dining room window. Bedrooms are clean, pine-bedded and old-fashioned – not for style fanatics – with comfortable chairs; one opens to the glorious garden. Cats and dogs doze, badgers visit, the peace is a balm. *Minimum stay two nights. Dogs welcome to sleep in the lobby.*

Price	From £66.
Rooms	2: 1 double, 1 twin/double sharing bath (let to same party only).
Meals	Pub 5-minute walk across fields, 1 mile by road.
Closed	Christmas.
Directions	From Clee Hill, south for Knowbury. One mile, left Hope Bagot Lane, second right Cumberley Lane. Under bridge, past Cumberley, 100 yds to The Croft Cottage.

Elizabeth & David Hatchell
The Croft Cottage, Cumberley Lane,
Knowbury, Ludlow SY8 3LJ

Tel	01584 890664
Email	garden@croftcottagebedandbreakfast.co.uk
Web	www.croftcottagebedandbreakfast.co.uk

Travel Club Offer. See page 290.

Ethical Collection: Food.
See page 294.

Entry 74 Map 2

Pennard House

The garden: Sweeping lawns, mature trees, a 14th-century church below, a south-facing suntrap terrace, a formal rose garden, pools and curious topiary... Pennard House is one of those dreamy landscape gardens straight from the pages of P G Wodehouse. All seems serene, graceful, easy – and on a grand scale – yet a huge amount of time and hard work has gone into developing and restoring the grounds of Susie's family home. Shady laurels and yews were the dominant feature until the couple launched a clearance and restoration campaign after taking advice from expert friends. Pennard House has, in fact, two gardens within a garden, divided by a little lane. There are the open, sunny lawns of the house garden and, across the road, a second garden with clipped hedges, a formal rose garden and that inviting spring-fed pool which in turn feeds a series of ponds below. Don't miss the witty topiary cottage, rabbit and other creatures which the gardener has created over the years. Susie always has some new project afoot – a recent success was ripping out cotoneaster below the terrace and replacing it with a formally-planted combination of rosemary, roses and lavender. Knock a few balls around on the grass court, swim in the crystal clear water of the pool, or simply stroll among the colour, the scents and the blooms.

The house: Pennard has been in Susie's family since the 17th century – the cellars date from then and the superstructure is stately, lofty and Georgian. Multi-lingual Martin runs an antiques business from here and he and Susie obviously enjoy having guests in their home. You have the run of the library, drawing room, magnificent billiard room, 60-acre orchard, meadows, woods, grass tennis court and six acres of garden with a spring-fed pool (swim with the newts). Bedrooms are large and have good views; one is oval with a corner bath in the room. Although this is a big house it still feels warm and comfortably lived in.

Price	From £90. Singles from £45.
Rooms	3: 1 double, 1 twin; 1 twin/double with separate bath/shower.
Meals	Pub 2 miles.
Closed	Rarely.
Directions	From Shepton Mallet south on A37, through Pylle, over hill & next right to East Pennard. After 500 yds, right & follow lane past church to T-junc. at very top. House on left.

Martin & Susie Dearden
Pennard House, East Pennard,
Shepton Mallet BA4 6TP

Tel	01749 860266
Fax	01749 860700
Email	susie.d@ukonline.co.uk

Travel Club Offer. See page 290.

Townsend Farm

The garden: An exquisite garden, and all designed by Helen; the only inherited features are some huge yew topiaries. It has taken three years so far, and there are always more plans afoot, but these two acres – all facing the house – have been transformed. From the house you step onto a grass terrace where the vast, neat yews lurk, then down steps to another terrace and the stylish rill surrounded by wide gravel paths and with an oak gazebo at either end. This culminates in a pool, painted black to make the water more reflective: all this hard landscaping, perfectly designed, is softened with large herbaceous beds. Down the ha-ha and into a large mown meadow area with newly planted fruit trees surrounded by a field hedge of indigenous species and honeysuckle. At the bottom is a dreamy lake with a boat and an island and moorhens and coots; occasionally deer visit if you sit still for long enough. To one side of the house is a neat knot garden, all in white, and to the other side a walled vegetable garden with rectangular raised beds and a fruit cage. Here the hens have a deeply smart house in which to lay your breakfast egg. Glorious planting brings it all together: 1000 alliums, 1000 daffodils and dozens of trees. This is clever stuff.

The house: In a charming part of Somerset, with quiet villages and small market towns, this Ham stone 17th-century farmhouse is flagstone floored, wooden shuttered and mullion windowed to perfection. Inside has a more modern, crisp feel with grey/blue walls, squashy pale sofas and warm carpets. Bedrooms are elegant with good antiques, thick mattresses, gay fabrics and contemporary limestone bathrooms. Treats include homemade cookies, a decanter of sherry, fresh flowers artfully arranged. Equally stylish Helen gives you dreamy breakfasts, like smoked salmon and scrambled eggs, sweet or savoury pancakes, excellent coffee. Lovely. *Unsuitable for children.*

Price	£80. Singles £60.
Rooms	3: 2 doubles; 1 double with separate bath.
Meals	Pub 50 yds.
Closed	November-March.
Directions	A303 to Cartgate roundabout. A3088 south for 1 mile. Turn for Montacute, through village until sign for Lower Odcombe and Masons Arms. House is 2nd on left after 30mph sign. Wrought iron railings along front.

Travel Club Offer. See page 290.

Helen Dickson
Townsend Farm,
51 Lower Odcombe, Yeovil BA22 8TX

Tel   01935 862523
Email   helenmariadickson@btinternet.com

Carpenters

The garden: Gardening has been a lifelong passion with Christabel; she and lawnsman/pruner Mike are an excellent team. When they came to Carpenters 18 years ago they inherited a highly-managed, sloping garden enclosed by local hamstone walls with views to Ham and the Chiselborough hills. Over the years they have added unusual trees and shrubs to create height and structure; the catalpa they planted at the start is now large enough to sit under on a summer's evening — and enjoy a glass of Mike's delicious homemade wine. (His half-acre vineyard lies just beyond.) Formally shaped borders have been informally planted with hardy geraniums, shrub roses and as many pinks and other favourites as Christabel can pack in, while striking architectural plants, like acanthus and phormiums, tower above. A climbing frame is festooned with 'Sander's White Rambler', clematis and honeysuckle. Mike keeps the lawns in pristine condition, prunes trees and shrubs and has carved a straggling yew hedge into dramatic, sentinel-like shapes beyond the double borders. From the first spring flowers to the late autumn blaze of acer, this garden holds your interest. The sole exception to Mike and Christabel's organic rule is the occasional anti-slug offensive in their vegetable garden. *RHS, HPS.*

The house: Down a sleepy lane in a hamstone village lies a house heavy with history. A purple wisteria embraces the front door of Carpenters which dates from the 1700s and, until the 1930s, was a carpenter's home; the sunny sitting room where guests are welcomed was the workshop. Christabel picks fresh flowers from the garden for the house and, on the day we visited, deliciously scented daphne cuttings in the hall. All is immaculately cared for with soft-coloured carpets and pretty wallpapers hung in bright bedrooms. Breakfast on fruits from the garden, home-baked bread and Christabel's tasty yogurt. *Children by arrangement.*

Price	£80. Singles £45.
Rooms	2: 1 twin, 1 single both sharing bath.
Meals	Pub/restaurant 5-minute walk.
Closed	24 December-2 January.
Directions	From A303, A356 for Crewkerne. Ignore turn to Stoke-sub-Hamdon; on for 1 mile to x-roads. Left into Norton-sub-Hamdon, 1st right into Higher St. Up to bend, straight through gate by small greenhouse.

Mike & Christabel Cumberlege
Carpenters,
Norton-sub-Hamdon TA14 6SN

Tel	01935 881255
Fax	01935 881255
Email	mikecumbo@hotmail.com
Web	www.carpentersbb.co.uk

Travel Club Offer. See page 290.

Hartwood House

The garden: This peaceful garden is set within a sheltered glade of beech trees – a glorious setting. It is a garden of many parts. From the house you gaze over the croquet lawn down past an unusual selection of young flourishing shrubs and trees to a magnificent 300-year-old oak. Wander back up the woodland path, edged with primulas and lilies of the valley, through camellias, rhododendrons and azaleas (and hydrangeas in summer) to the formal garden of circles. Here is lush planting within a planned colour scheme. In the centre, an armillary within a stone circle surrounded by pillars up which grow 'Dublin Bay' roses. Duck under a rose and clematis arch to find yourself in David's vegetable garden: a joy to look at and a joy to work in. Here, narrow brick-edged borders guard vegetables of every description, a circular greenhouse nurtures tomatoes, melons, peppers and aubergines, there are beds for asparagus and raspberries, and a fine runner-bean arch – Rosemary's favourite. And there's a large and splendid davidia, whose seeds are now growing to provide a half avenue up the drive. In spring, an old and prolific mulberry tree protects a carpet of fritillaries, while the bank beside the yew is drenched with snowdrops and the field is bright with daffodils.

The house: Having run 'Gardens of Somerset' tours, David and Rosemary are experts at both looking after their guests (tea and homemade cakes on arrival, delicious breakfasts) and showing them West Somerset's loveliest corners. The house exudes warmth and comfort, and guests have a large sitting room, a cosy wood-burner, a sprawl of easy chairs, and stacks of books and jigsaw puzzles. Bedrooms are comfortable, traditional and spacious with good mattresses, fresh flowers and garden views. Nights are exceptionally quiet: you may hear owls and the occasional vixen. Immaculately kept and everything works properly – a joy in itself.

Price	£70. Singles from £35.
Rooms	4: 3 twins/doubles; 1 single with separate bath.
Meals	Occasional dinner £25. Pub 1 mile.
Closed	Occasionally.
Directions	From Taunton, A358, for 9 miles, then left signed Crowcombe Station. Over railway bridge; right at T-junction. Last house on left after about 400 yds.

David & Rosemary Freemantle
Hartwood House, Crowcombe
Heathfield, Taunton TA4 4BS

Tel	01984 667202
Fax	01984 667508
Email	hartwoodhouse@hotmail.com

Ethical Collection: Community.
See page 294.

Binham Grange

The garden: Marie, a passionate gardener, has been involved with the restoration of Aberglasney Gardens, and she has created her own from scratch; about one-and-a-half acres around the house falling out into 300-acres of lush Somerset landscape. This young garden has been planted to excite the senses and to enhance conditions for wildlife in an ecological way. There's a formal parterre to the east of the house, and a south-facing terrace which overlooks the cutting garden – a riot of colour from cosmos, nigella, calendula, roses, night-scented stocks and sweet peas. Beautiful organic vegetables are grown for the kitchen from Italian seeds; "to be a good cook you need a good garden" says Marie. To the west is the main terrace, a great spot to have afternoon tea or enjoy an evening drink while looking over the gardens to Exmoor and the West Somerset Steam Railway. Stroll round the part-walled garden with its pretty walls of red sandstone and blue lias, discover the orchard, look for otters in the river, watch the cows come across the field for milking... if you are lucky you will spot geese flying overhead. One guest described this as paradise.

The house: Set between the Quantock and Brendon hills, and with the coastal path nearby, Old Cleeve is an excellent area for walking, and this place is perfect if you prefer a bit of luxury when you haul your boots off. The stunning Jacobean manor house has been modernised with great care: one bedroom is enormous with its own little sitting area and table for private breakfasts; both have super views, smart carpets, wind-up radios and rather posh bathrooms. Marie and her daughter Victoria are great cooks and all food is local, much is organic; you eat in what was probably the Great Hall, with a distant ceiling. Impressive.

Price	£100–£140. Singles £80.
Rooms	2: 1 double, 1 suite.
Meals	Dinner, 4 courses, £30. Restaurant 3 miles.
Closed	February.
Directions	A39 to Minehead, then right at crossroads after Washford to Blue Anchor. Past Old Cleeve & house is on left.

Marie Thomas
Binham Grange, Old Cleeve,
Minehead TA24 6HX

Tel	01984 640056
Email	mariethomas@btconnect.com
Web	www.binhamgrange.co.uk

The Old Priory

The garden: Jane Forshaw's bewitching walled garden in the beautiful Somerset town of Dunster is a wonderfully personal creation. You'll discover a bounteous blend of formal touches with shrubs, small trees and climbers which are allowed to express themselves freely. The garden perfectly complements her ancient priory home... a place of reflection, seclusion and peace. A tall mimosa greets you at the little gate on a lane overlooked by the Castle, mature espaliered fruit trees line the garden path and then comes Jane's most formal touch, the square, knee-high hedged box garden. The shrubs for this were rescued from the Castle's 'Dream Garden' when the National Trust abandoned it because they thought it would be too labour-consuming to maintain. Jane piled as many of the uprooted shrubs as she could into the back of a van, heeled them into some empty land and later arranged them into their present design. Informally planted herbaceous borders and a small lawn in front of the house complete the picture. Through an archway you wander into the church grounds with stunning long beds which Jane helps maintain. When the writer Simon Jenkins drew up his list of the best churches in England, Dunster received star billing and the grounds did even better. He described it as the most delightful church garden in England... see if you agree.

The house: Ancient, rambling, beamed and flagstoned, Jane's 12th-century home is as much a haven for reflection and good company today as it was to the monastic community who once lived here. Both house and hostess are dignified, unpretentious and friendly; Jane adds her own special flair with artistic touches here and there, and books and dogs for company. There are funky Venetian-red walls in the low-ceilinged, time-worn living room with its magnificent stone 14th-century fireplace and, in one bedroom, decoratively painted wardrobe doors. The big bedroom – undulating oaken floor and four-poster – is deeply authentic.

Price	£80–£90. Singles by arrangement.
Rooms	3: 1 twin, 1 four-poster; 1 double with separate shower.
Meals	Restaurants/pubs 5-minute walk.
Closed	Christmas.
Directions	From A39 into Dunster, right at blue sign 'Unsuitable for Goods Vehicles'. Follow until church; house adjoined.

Jane Forshaw
The Old Priory,
Dunster TA24 6RY

Tel	01643 821540
Web	www.theoldpriory-dunster.co.uk

Travel Club Offer. See page 290.

Ethical Collection: Food.
See page 294.

Manor House

The garden: When the house was rebuilt in 1708 the garden was devised. The house sits on a north-facing slope and the three-acre garden runs out on the south side into a series of five terraces, each one topped by neatly clipped yews. Chris inherited the house, then set to expand and improve the garden into a place of exploration, rest and relaxation; many seats are dotted here and there for lovely views over the Weaver hills. There is humour and quirk too: an extensive perennial border sports a huge stone table which was once part of the entrance to Lancaster's municipal baths, and an old goods railway carriage is now a garden summer house. Yew trees, hedge walls and terraces mean that you have to wander to see the full value of the garden, and guests are encouraged to stay as long as they want. Planting includes lots of evergreens with splashes of summer colour, and the odd pretty weed – Chris will brook no spraying at all. This means the wildlife is abundant, from birds and butterflies to hedgehogs and squirrels. The old cow lane is now a mown path, and remains of old farm buildings have been left covered with ivy and with statues placed among them. A lovely, interesting garden filled with fun, and very peaceful to sit in.

The house: A working rare-breed farm in an area of great beauty, a Jacobean farmhouse with oodles of history. Behind mullioned windows is an interior crammed with curios and family pieces, panelled walls and wonky floors... hurl a log on the fire and watch it roar. Rooms with views have four-posters; one bathroom flaunts rich red antique fabrics. Chris and Margaret serve perfect breakfasts (home-grown tomatoes, sausages and bacon from their outdoor-reared pigs, eggs from their hens) and give you the run of the garden with tennis and croquet. There are two springer spaniels and one purring cat. Heaven.

Price	£54–£65. Singles £34–£45.
Rooms	4: 3 four-posters, 1 double.
Meals	Pub/restaurant 1.5 miles.
Closed	Christmas.
Directions	From Uttoxeter, B5030 for Rocester. Beyond JCB factory, left onto B5031. At T-junc. after church, right onto B5032. 1st left for Prestwood. Farm 0.75 miles on right over crest of hill, through arch.

Chris & Margaret Ball
Manor House, Prestwood,
Denstone, Uttoxeter ST14 5DD

Tel	01889 590415
Fax	01335 342198
Email	cm_ball@yahoo.co.uk
Web	www.4posteraccom.com

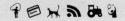

Entry 81   Map 6

Abbey House

The garden: Fine old trees — oaks, limes, beeches and weeping willows — dignify the three acres of garden and seven of meadowland surrounding Sue's Victorian rectory on the site of an ancient abbey; evidence of her love of gardening — and her talent for it — is all around you. Early flowering yellow banksia climbs the front of the house, fighting for the limelight with the *Clematis montana* that tumbles around the door. The heated swimming pool (which you may use if you ask) lies enclosed in a sheltered suntrap surrounded by trellises of fragrant honeysuckle, jasmine and trachelospermum. Several passion flowers run riot and there's a gravel bed for hot-and dry-lovers: Japanese banana, agapanthus, verdant bamboo and interesting ornamental grasses. Plenty of new shrubs have gone in this year and the shrub walk also parades many mature plants including viburnum and rubus 'Benenden'. This is a thoroughly peaceful space to amble around: sit and contemplate a game of croquet under the magnificent copper beech, admire the swans and ducks in the lovely pond lined with flag irises — best viewed from a picturesque arched wooden bridge. Then wander at will in the woodland with its early carpet of snowdrops and aconites; further afield you will find a small flock of sheep and assorted fowl.

The house: A spectacular arrival. Find a handsome, listed, Dutch-gabled house (1846) fronted by an impressive fishpond — the monks ate well here — upon which black swans glide. On land, the peacocks lord it over the chickens. Sue's welcome is warm and easy, her bedrooms simply and comfortably arranged, each with a couple of armchairs and garden or pond views. High ceilings and large windows make for a light, tranquil atmosphere. Settle down in front of the fire in the guest drawing room, or wander out through French windows to the shrub walk. Breakfast sausages and bacon are local; the eggs are from just outside.

Price	£60. Singles £30.
Rooms	3: 2 doubles; 1 twin with separate bath.
Meals	Pubs 2.5 miles.
Closed	Christmas & New Year.
Directions	From Earl Soham A1120, to Monk Soham for approx. 2 miles. Right fork at top of hill, house 300 yds on left after bend and opp. Church Farm.

Mrs Sue Bagnall
Abbey House, Monk Soham,
Framlingham IP13 7EN

Tel	01728 685225
Email	sue@abbey-house.net
Web	www.abbey-house.net

The Old Butchers Shop

The garden: When Sarah took over the garden four years ago it was completely overgrown and had been neglected for 15 years. So she started from scratch and has cleverly designed and made virtually everything you see. On sunny days you can breakfast on the paved courtyard near the house, surrounded by colourful pots and an attractive lead water urn. Through a rose and clematis arch you will find the herb garden in wooden raised beds; a delight to wander through on warm evenings, it also has a swing seat overlooking the church. Another rose arch with two Conference pears trained over it takes you to the bottom garden and a wider, open space. Surrounded by herbaceous borders full of sand-loving plants (peonies, lupins, delphiniums and sweet peas), and with plenty of places to sit, there are rose beds and a pond packed with lilies, frogs, toads and newts – and a shallow, pebbled end for birds and even mallards. In her robust vegetable garden Sarah grows rhubarb, raspberries, blackcurrants and tomatoes; apart from one rowan, all the other trees have been recently planted and are mainly ornamental. Sarah gardens because she adores being surrounded by beautiful flowers and greenery. She loves sharing it, too.

The house: Artist Sarah has cleverly converted this old butcher's shop: you're right on the main street of an undisturbed brick and timber estuary village, a hop from the sea for birdwatching or walks. Bedrooms, not huge, are pretty and light with proper linen on supremely comfortable beds and views over the maturing garden or the street and fine Norman church. Two happy cats lie comatose in the drawing room with its gay kilims and bright checks, books jostle for space with pictures. Sarah is laid-back and fun and cooks a mean breakfast: homemade yogurt and stewed fruits, local kippers. Snape for music lovers is close by.

Price	£65–£75. Singles from £45.
Rooms	3: 2 twins/doubles; 1 twin/double with separate bath/shower.
Meals	Pubs/restaurants within 5-min. walk.
Closed	Rarely.
Directions	From A12, signs to Orford. Left-hand bend after King's Head pub towards quay. House on opposite side of road with blue door. Park in Market Sq.

Travel Club Offer. See page 290.

Mrs Sarah Holland
The Old Butchers Shop, 111 Church St,
Orford, Woodbridge IP12 2LL

Tel	01394 450517
Fax	01394 459436
Email	sarah@oldbutchers-orford.co.uk
Web	www.oldbutchers-orford.co.uk

Shoelands House

The garden: The original front gardens were formal, as revealed by a painting from 1793. Sarah and Clive, having raised their family here, are now recreating this design to some extent, in four flower beds around a small terracotta urn. Over the years the common hardy geraniums have been replaced by more unusual plants – the garden is at its most colourful in late summer. The beds to the side of the path leading to the front door have been planted with David Austin roses and lavender, yellow species tulips and other peach-coloured flowers, then formally edged with box. The garden at the back – where a 16th-century dovecote once stood – is divided by a mellow brick wall, against which a contoured bed has been planted; the delphiniums are lovely in July. Further beds have been laid out in a goose-foot pattern, one grassy path leading to a willow, another to a bridge over the stream, a third to the end of the garden and an old box hedge. Small flowering trees and shrubs underplanted with perennials ensure colour much of the year. The medieval small lake – or big pond – has been revived in 1999, filled with water lilies and edged with bullrushes, while the original greenhouses have been allocated to the hens – the source of your breakfast eggs.

The house: Behind the beautiful brickwork façade, history oozes from carved panel and creaking stair. The dining room, with its cross beams and stunning oak door, dates from 1616: Sarah and Clive know all the history. Ecclesiastical paintings, family photos, embroidered sofas, tapestry rugs; the décor is endearingly haphazard, nothing matches and the house feels loved. Bedrooms have white walls and beams, and big old radiators for heat; old-fashioned bathrooms are papered and carpeted. You are peacefully between Puttenham and Seale villages, just off the 'Hog's Back' – blissfully quiet. Readers love this place.

Price	£85. Singles from £60.
Rooms	2 twins/doubles.
Meals	Occasional supper. Pub/restaurant 1 mile.
Closed	Rarely.
Directions	On Seale-Puttenham road, halfway between Guildford & Farnham, just south of the Hog's Back.

Clive & Sarah Webster
Shoelands House, Seale,
Farnham GU10 1HL

Tel	01483 810213
Fax	01483 811433
Email	clive@clivewebster.co.uk

Entry 84 Map 3

Nurscombe Farmhouse

The garden: No fewer than 36 Leylandii trees had to be banished when Jane took over. Once they had gone, a garden, walled on three sides, was revealed. Since then she has worked steadily to achieve a true cottage-garden effect. Working on sandy soil, her aim is for it to look "casually cared for, not too formal". She has achieved this – brilliantly. A mixed herbaceous border behind the house has random repeat planting at either end. 'Iceberg' roses on a bargate wall provide a backdrop for a sloping border with a blue, pink and magenta colour scheme; at the back are *Crambe cordifolia* and pretty cranesbill. In the vegetable garden, where there's a fine old wooden greenhouse, a tayberry flourishes against the back wall and herbs, root vegetables, beans, courgettes and sugar snaps grow. Fruit from the old apple and plum trees sometimes figures on the breakfast menu, along with wild mushrooms and nuts. There's a new rose arch, and the garden, set in 40 acres of gentle hills (bluebell woods, a trout-filled lake, a rowing boat), is visited by birds and the occasional hedgehog, fox or badger. Jane also organises private tours to local gardens designed by Gertrude Jekyll in collaboration with Edwin Lutyens (see her website).

The house: It is blissfully peaceful. You enter through an old archway, past irises and heavy wooden gates, to discover a 15th-century farmhouse. Beautifully restored barns and stables are scattered around; sheep munch in the fields below. You can slump in front of a fire in the drawing room, sleep quietly in simple, characterful bedrooms with well-worn carpets, striped wallpaper and long views; frill-free bathrooms are in traditional working order. A proper farmhouse breakfast sets you up for a visit to Loseley Park, the Norman church at Compton or a country walk. *Minimum stay two nights at weekends.*

Price	From £80. Singles from £45.
Rooms	2: 1 double, 1 twin, each with bath & separate wc.
Meals	Pub/restaurant 1 mile.
Closed	Rarely.
Directions	At roundabout in Bramley on A281, right up Snowdenham Lane. One mile uphill, house on right opposite white 5-bar gate. Drive through archway into courtyard.

Mrs Jane Fairbank
Nurscombe Farmhouse,
Snowdenham Lane, Bramley GU5 0DB

Tel	01483 892242
Fax	01483 892242
Email	fairbank@onetel.com
Web	www.nurscombe.com

Entry 85   Map 3

Lordington House

The garden: The arrival is dramatic, a gentle rise, with – in spring – a sea of daffodils to either side; you slip between two stone pillars that appear to lean slightly outwards to allow you in. Emerge onto pea gravel in front of this truly beautiful house. The first impression of the garden is – bizarrely given its age – one of modernity; the crisp green wall of neatly sculpted golden yew and tall pines strike a contemporary note. Hedges and lawn live at the rear, rubbing shoulders with huge old stone walls and another pair of splendid gateposts which lead to the lime avenue, through which you may spot horses – bucolic bliss. A cherub waves from one wall and the view stretches effortlessly away, Long borders romp with low-growing aromatic shrubs, interspersed with pelargoniums, lilies, anemones and osteospermum. In the spring, the beds are bright with tulips; there are some old and interesting trees including a black mulberry and a paperbark maple. Well behaved vegetables sit in their rows, hundreds of cuttings are reared annually in the greenhouses, there are lovely places to sit with a glass of wine and a good book, and – for real gardeners – Audrey will be a treat to talk to. Overhead, buzzards wheel and mew.

The house: On a sunny slope of the Ems valley, life ticks by peacefully as it has always done... apart from a touch of turbulence in the 16th century. The house is vast and impressive, with majestic views past clipped yew and pillared gates to the AONB beyond. Inside is engagingly old-fashioned with a few quirky flare-ups like a hand-painted harlequin design in the hall. Find Edwardian beds with proper bedspreads, carpeted Sixties-style bathrooms, shepherdess wallpapers up and over wardrobe doors. Tea cosies at breakfast, big log fires and a panelled drawing room. Bring your woolly jumper. *Children over five welcome.*

Price	From £90. Singles from £45.
Rooms	4: 1 double; 1 twin/double with separate bath/shower; 1 double, 1 single sharing bath/shower.
Meals	Dinner £20. Packed lunch from £5. Pub 1 mile.
Closed	Rarely.
Directions	Lordington (marked on some road maps) west side of B2146, 6 miles south of South Harting, 0.5 miles south of Walderton. Enter thro' white railings by letterbox; fork right after bridge.

Mr & Mrs John Hamilton
Lordington House, Lordington,
Chichester PO18 9DX

Tel	01243 375862
Fax	01243 375862
Email	audreyhamilton@onetel.com

Travel Club Offer. See page 290.

Entry 86 Map 3

73 Sheepdown Drive

The garden: From the back of the house the view across the small valley to the South Downs is outstanding. Since taking on this sloping, 60-foot garden seven years ago, Angela has transformed a tricky plot. Visible in its entirety from the windows above, the planting has been cleverly designed with many hidden corners. The area has been divided across the middle, with the view from the top end framed by the herbaceous borders that curve down either side. A central oval bed conceals an entrance through to the lower part of the garden and from here plants frame the view without obscuring it: a prunus gives height and shade to one side; azaleas, rhododendrons and weigela will be pruned as they grow to maintain a particular size. Owners of small gardens will delight to find one here with which they can comfortably identify. A gate at the bottom leads to a network of footpaths that lead you around much of the area without having to resort to the car. Walk round to the town – heaven for antiques-lovers – or down through the fields to the pub in Byworth for supper. *NGS Vice-President.*

The house: A short walk from the centre of lovely Petworth, number 73 lies in a quiet, 1970s cul-de-sac and has glorious green views. Once chairman of the National Gardens Scheme, now a vice-president, Angela has a background that will fascinate anyone who loves gardens; she has a particular insight into the gardens and nurseries of Sussex. Bedrooms are fresh and pretty, with good pictures, well-dressed beds and views; you eat at a long Jacobean oak table and the sunny conservatory is a super place to enjoy a book overlooking the garden. Handy for Chichester's theatre, glorious Goodwood and Petworth House.

Price	From £60. Singles from £35.
Rooms	2 twins sharing bath & shower.
Meals	Pub/restaurant 10-minute walk.
Closed	Christmas & New Year.
Directions	From Petworth on A283. Sheepdown Drive east of village centre.

Mrs Angela Azis
73 Sheepdown Drive,
Petworth GU28 0BX

Tel	01798 342269
Fax	01798 342269

Entry 87   Map 3

Pindars

The garden: The weeds towered above the children when Jocelyne and Clive bought the field 40 years ago. Once the house was built, they had £5 left for creating the garden – from scratch. Over the years, they have softened and transformed the square lines of the field into a magical place of curves and corners, open vistas and secret places. Everything – terraces, swimming pool, flint wall with fountain – has been designed and built by them. They have also planted about 100 trees, including poplars, birches, eucalyptus, oaks and cherries, some of which are felled as necessary. Jocelyne's particular love is the *Acer platanoides*, fully grown and superb; another special tree is a big chestnut, reared from a conker and nursed back to life by Clive after it was split in half by the 1987 gale. The borders are a mix of shrubs and perennials with some summer bedding (though Jocelyne also fills pots with annuals, which she can then move around). She plants for foliage colour, shape and height in large, naturally shaped splodges. If plants seed themselves, they are often allowed to stay, giving a relaxed, unstudied effect. Swallows nest in the garage every year and green woodpeckers are frequent visitors.

The house: A beaming welcome from Jocelyne sets the tone. She and Clive are excellent company and their 1960s house is warm, well-loved and lived-in. The road is busy but the guest sitting room faces the beautiful gardens, as do two of the bedrooms; the other surveys Arundel Castle. Bedrooms are light and comfortable, bathrooms are white and pristine. Books, magazines, watercolours and two Burmese cats complete the happy picture. Jocelyne's cooking is imaginative so breakfast and dinner will be delightful – and the just-finished Jacobean garden at Arundel is wonderfully close. *Minimum stay two nights preferred.*

Price	£65–£75. Singles £45–£50.
Rooms	3: 1 double; 1 double, 1 twin with separate bathroom (let to same party only).
Meals	Dinner £20–£28. Pub 0.5 miles.
Closed	Rarely.
Directions	1 mile south of A27 on A284. House on left after 1st sharp right-hand bend.

Jocelyne & Clive Newman
Pindars, Lyminster,
Arundel BN17 7QF

Tel	01903 882628
Fax	01938 882628
Email	pindars@tiscali.co.uk
Web	www.pindars.co.uk

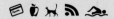

Travel Club Offer. See page 290.

Ethical Collection: Community; Food.
See page 294.

www. holywellbarn. com

Copyhold Hollow

The garden: As pretty as a picture. Protected on one side by an ancient box hedge and fed by a natural spring, the garden is literally 'in' the hollow with the house. Frances has developed the whole thing herself over the last 16 years creating two acres of joy. Water lovers paddle happily around the stream's edge including flag irises, astilbes, unusual and prettily marked red and yellow mimulus, hostas and *Crocosmia lucifer*. There is an innovative green Giverny-like bridge, over which is fixed an arched sweet-chestnut tunnel now covered in wisteria, clematis, roses and jasmine. There's another arch further up the brick path, smothered in *Trachelospermum asiaticum*, roses and clematis. Walk through mixed borders to a patio – eating out here is fun – and feel protected from the weather: you are tucked in beneath a natural hanger of mature beech and oak trees and a giant redwood. Behind the house is a bank up to the tree line, with paths, camellias, rhododendrons and azaleas. The soil is acid and very heavy clay so not easy to work but it all looks perfect. Come at any time for something special; in the spring the garden is especially merry with wild daffodils, snowdrops, bluebells and wild orchids.

The house: The 16th-century house hides behind a 1,000-year-old box hedge, its land delineated by an ancient field boundary. First a farm, then an ale house, Copyhold Hollow seems small from the outside but opens into a quirky interior of exposed timbers. Frances did the restoration herself, and coaxed the garden and woodland back to life: the results are charming. The guests' dining room and sitting room with inglenook fireplace are beamed, uncluttered and cheerful; bedrooms have goosedown duvets and wonderful views. Your lively, independent hostess has masses of info on walks and cycle routes.

Price	£80–£100. Singles £50–£55.
Rooms	3: 1 double, 1 twin, 1 single. Extra beds available.
Meals	Dinner, 3 courses, £34–£39 (minimum 4 people). Pub/restaurant 0.5 miles.
Closed	Rarely.
Directions	M23, exit junc.10a; B2036 for Cuckfield. There, over mini r'bout. At 2nd r'bout, left into Ardingly Rd; right at 3rd r'bout into Hanlye Lane; left at T-junc., 1st right for Ardingly; 0.5 miles on right.

Frances Druce
Copyhold Hollow, Copyhold Lane,
Borde Hill, Haywards Heath RH16 1XU

Tel	01444 413265
Email	bbgl@copyholdhollow.co.uk
Web	www.copyholdhollow.co.uk

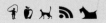 Travel Club Offer. See page 290.

Ethical Collection: Environment;
Community; Food. See page 294.

Entry 89   Map 3

Stone House

The garden: Chatsworth in miniature. Five and a half acres of sweeping lawns, two lakes, 'hot' and 'cool' borders, an 18th-century rose garden to match the front of the house, a tunnel of apples and pears, an avenue of lime trees by falling pools and, perhaps most outstanding of all, a 1728 walled kitchen garden quartered by brick paths. Jane is a veg and herb guru, great-great-granddaughter of the designer who laid out some of Castle Howard and Kew, and modestly thrilled by her plot. One of her passions is colour, and she often plants in blocks for impact. The short border brims with yellows, whites and blues, the 100ft-long one with pinks, reds and golds, and the vegetable garden has a glorious palette: 'Red Rubine' brussel sprouts alongside grey-green 'Cavallo Nero', radicchio nudging yellow-green Chinese cabbage, marigolds cosying up to cornflowers, and dozens of unusual 'cut and come again' salads. Trees include a black poplar (rare for the south), a white mulberry and a magnificent Japanese maple. How does she achieve such abundance? Jane – supported by a delightful bunch of part-time gardeners – gives the thumbs up to comfrey manure, grit (tons of it) for a clay soil, mushroom compost to keep down weeds and a polytunnel for the veg.

The house: This part-Tudor, part-Georgian house has been in the family since 1492, its windows gazing over gardens and parkland that have been cherished for centuries. Peter and Jane are gentle and charming and the six bedrooms are period stunners: floral canopies and matching drapes, grand mirrors, family antiques. Delectable meals (game from the estate, vegetables, herbs and fruits from the gardens, wines from the cellars) are served at crisply dressed tables. Peter guides you to the gardens and castles of Sussex and Kent, Jane, a Master Chef, rustles up peerless picnics for Glyndebourne. *Children over eight welcome.*

Price	£135–£260 Singles £110–£140.
Rooms	8: 4 twins/doubles, 2 four-posters, 1 suite; 1 twin with separate bath.
Meals	Lunch & dinner £27.95.
Closed	Christmas & New Year.
Directions	From Heathfield, B2096; 4th turning on right, signed Rushlake Green. 2 miles down hill & up into village. 1st left by village green to x-roads; house on far left, signed.

Peter & Jane Dunn
Stone House, Rushlake Green,
Heathfield TN21 9QJ

Tel	01435 830553
Fax	01435 830726
Web	www.stonehousesussex.co.uk

Travel Club Offer. See page 290.

Entry 90   Map 4

Hailsham Grange

The garden: There is a quiet element of the unexpected in Noel's garden, which is as stunning as the house. Perhaps it's because of his upbringing in New Zealand, at a time when many gardens still clung to traditional English patterns but were enlivened by native exotics. Here, within a formal framework of box, yew and hornbeam hedging, Noel has created a whole series of gardens, yet within the formality, has mixed and juxtaposed his plants in an informal and original way. The effect is relaxed, romantic and subtly different. Separate areas are themed for colour – of foliage or flower – with plants chosen for scent and grouped in swathes so they blend into each other. All this has been achieved in the years since Noel took over Hailsham Grange. When he arrived, in 1988, he was presented with the challenge of a completely blank, one-acre canvas and is still constantly experimenting (the spring garden is where any that are doing badly are given their last chance – it's flourish or die!). There are several enticing spots to sit with an evening drink and contemplate all this beauty: a bench in the daffodil-filled spinney, a chair in the dell, and a seat in the enchanting gothic summerhouse. Look out for the unusual Plectranthus!

The house: Come for elegance and ease. Noel welcomes you into his lovely Queen 'Mary Anne' home (a vicarage built in 1701), set back from the road next to the church. No standing on ceremony here, despite the décor: classic English touched with chinoiserie in perfect keeping with the house. Busts on pillars, swathes of delicious chintz, books galore and bedrooms a treat; the four-poster and the double overlooking the garden share a cosy sitting room. Summery breakfasts are served on the flagged terrace, marmalades and jams on a silver salver. The town garden, with its box parterre and bank of cherry trees, is an equal joy.

Price	£95–£120. Singles from £60.
Rooms	4: 1 double, 1 four-poster. Coach house: 2 suites.
Meals	Pub/restaurants 300 yds.
Closed	Rarely.
Directions	From Hailsham High St, left into Vicarage Rd. House 200 yds on left. Park in adjacent coach yard.

Mr Noel Thompson
Hailsham Grange,
Hailsham BN27 1BL

Tel	01323 844248
Email	noel@hgrange.co.uk
Web	www.hailshamgrange.co.uk

Travel Club Offer. See page 290.

Little Worge Barn

The garden: An exciting new garden. Stephen and Susan are garden designers and have left behind a 15-year-long, much-admired creation to paint a different picture here. The broad canvas is the achingly gorgeous sweep of valleys and hills that surround the barn; the challenge: to create a one-acre garden that doesn't detract from such splendour, *and* is practical to manage. To the east and south of the barn are two sunny terraces for sitting out; to the north, a sloped grassed area with views to the Wealden hills. The south-facing terrace is home to a productive greenhouse and an elegant eating area where the warmth and shelter encourage salvias, euphorbias, penstemons, geraniums, cistus and hebe. On a more practical note a hen run and a device for water collection are witness to the 'working garden'. Further afield are acres of mature woodland, ancient blackthorn hedgerows laden with honeysuckle, broom and holly; the windy conditions on the crest lead to stunted oaks and hawthorns. If all this makes you long to improve your own horticultural credentials you can walk from here to Sarah Raven's gardening school at The Cutting Garden.

The house: Pootle down through Sugar Loaf Wood — where *Cold Comfort Farm* was filmed — to arrive at your own smart little cottage. Find a beamed, light-filled sitting room, a stylish bedroom and a tiny kitchen on full alert. Be brave and fend for yourselves, or arrange for delicious breakfasts and suppers to be brought to you. If you like, you can eat next door at Susan and Stephen's 17th-century barn (your hosts are great fun). So do your own thing — but make sure you walk these blessed hills and spot the six follies built by the local 1800s eccentric, Mad Jack Fuller. *No dogs allowed.*

Price	£70-£90.
Rooms	Cottage with 1 twin/double, sitting room & kitchen.
Meals	Pub 1.5 miles.
Closed	Christmas & New Year.
Directions	Turn by church in Burwash down School Hill. After 3 miles, right at crossroads into Willingford Lane. Left after 100 yds onto concrete farm track; follow track to thatched barn at end, 0.75 miles.

Susan & Stephen Moir
Little Worge Barn, Willingford Lane,
Brightling TN32 5HN

Tel	01424 838136
Email	moirconsult@btinternet.com

Knellstone House

The garden: The house is a mix of old and new; so too is the garden. Linda and Stuart inherited some lovely old trees, a wood once frequented by smugglers, a pond and a happy wisteria, then added their own personality and are continuing to do a lot more. The garden is in different sections: formal at the front, terraced and bowl-shaped at the back, with fabulous views to the sea. A parterre provides cut flowers and some fruit and vegetables; an old barn is being converted into a greenhouse. Linda has a love of grasses, shaped beds and striking plants, many in dark reds, oranges and whites. Everything curves here – gateways and steps – to match the bowl shape. For height there are vertical railway sleepers, and a minimalist courtyard with a reflection pool, steel girders and climbers. At the front, a formal garden is developing. Wildlife is abundant: kestrels lurk in the bowl, badgers bumble at night (and eat the Harlands' figs, mischievous things). The terrace around the house has good seating areas and there is a glass-covered veranda so you can admire the views all year round. Great Dixter, Sissinghurst and Pashley Manor are close, should you need further inspiration.

The house: The Harlands have a stunning old house, built as a hall in 1490, with sloping, solid oak floors, mullioned windows and rare dragon beams. Glorious views reach across the Brede valley to sheep and then the sea. No old style interiors; instead, a refreshingly modern and bright feel with buttermilk walls, contemporary furniture, good lighting – and an elegant collection of simple carved heads from all over the world. Bedrooms are crisp, bathrooms are modern with luxurious accessories; wallow in one and gaze down to the sea. Birdlife abounds, soft fruits are served, Rye is a very short drive.

Price	From £110.
Rooms	2: 1 double; 1 double with separate bath.
Meals	Pub 600 yds.
Closed	Occasionally.
Directions	At the end of an unmade-up drive off the B2089. Travelling east, 1.2 miles after Kings Head pub, turn right. Travelling west, 0.3 miles after The Plough pub turn left.

Linda & Stuart Harland
Knellstone House,
Udimore, Rye TN31 6AR

Tel	01797 222410
Email	info@knellstonehouse.co.uk
Web	www.knellstonehouse.co.uk

Ethical Collection: Community.
See page 294.

Entry 93   Map 4

Shrewley Pools Farm

The garden: Everything is exuberant and down-to-earth about Cathy — and so is her garden. Originally planted by her mother-in-law in the 70s, the specimen trees and shrubs remain the same, with climbers and herbaceous perennials allowed to romp freely through the season. Cathy describes it as a fragrant, romantic garden: roses ramble through trees, scented wisteria and honeysuckle weave over the porch, and old-fashioned shrub roses perfume the borders. Great masses of hellebores herald the spring, and 30 different varieties of hostas are protected by the bantams who potter around gobbling up slugs. She enthusiastically reels off names, affectionately describing colours and habits ("There's this lovely little iris in the rockery called 'Mourning Widow' with almost-black flowers and fine leaves..."). Her busy bed-and-breakfast business makes her practical about maintenance: they work hard in the garden at the beginning and end of the season, but leave everything to perform by itself during the summer. And that it surely does. Shrewley Pools is a working farm smothered with flora; you'll see 'New Dawn' roses in the yard and clematis 'Perle d'Azur' romping over the stables. Bring your fishing rod; the four-and-a-half acre lake is stocked with 10,000 carp.

The house: An early-17th-century beamed farmhouse on a mixed, arable-animal farm... breakfast couldn't be more farmhouse if it tried. There are Shrewley Pools' own bacon and bangers and organic eggs from next door. Log fires in the dining room, sitting room and hall, beams all over, charmingly irregular quarry-tiled floors, old family furniture and chintz. The twin is beamy, oak-floored and rugged. The family room has a generous king-size bed and a single bed, as well as a cot, and fat sheepskin rugs on a mahogany floor. This is a super place for families in summer — and children's teas and babysitting are easily arranged.

Price	From £55. Singles from £40.
Rooms	2: 1 family room (& cot), 1 twin.
Meals	Packed lunch £4. Child's high tea £4. Pub/restaurant 1.5 miles.
Closed	Christmas.
Directions	From M40 junc. 15, A46 for Coventry. Left onto A4177. 4.5 miles to Five Ways r'bout. 1st left, on for 0.75 miles; signed, opp. Farm Gate Poultry: track on left.

Cathy Dodd
Shrewley Pools Farm, Five Ways Road,
Haseley, Warwick CV35 7HB

Tel	01926 484315
Email	cathydodd@hotmail.co.uk
Web	www.shrewleypoolsfarm.co.uk

Travel Club Offer. See page 290.

Entry 94   Map 3

Salford Farm House

The garden: An enchanting garden that flows from one space to another, studded with rare and interesting plants. It is also divided by a wing of the house, so you pass under an open-sided brick and timber barn (a wonderful seated area for lazy summer days) to cross from one side to the other. The garden has matured well thanks to a packed planting of roses, shrubs and herbaceous perennials: Jane has an artist's eye. Beautiful arrangements of plants in pots and a square, formal pond populated by water fowl reveal her talent. Clever curvy lawns, as smooth as bowling greens, dotted with island beds, give the illusion of space. There is always another corner to peek around and plenty of height: a pretty gazebo covered in clematis, weathered deer-fencing screens, a large pergola the length of one wall. There are natural old log sculptures for fun and urns of floaty pink geum; leggy metal seedpods add a contemporary touch. A garden for all seasons, with tulips in spring (heaps of them), peonies, pinks and penstemmon in summer, chrysanthemums and asters in autumn. Richard is MD of Hillers, a mile down the road – an award-winning fruit farm, café, shop and display garden from which you can buy all the inspiration you need to take home.

The house: Beautiful within, handsome without. Thanks to subtle colours, oak beams and lovely old pieces, Jane has achieved a seductive combination of comfort and style. A flagstoned hallway and an old rocking horse, ticking clocks, beeswax and fresh flowers: this house is well-loved. Jane was a ballet dancer, Richard has green fingers and runs a fruit farm nearby. Dinners are superb: meat and game from the Ragley Estate, delicious fruits in season. Bedrooms have a soft, warm elegance and flat-screen TVs, bathrooms are spotless and welcoming, views are to garden or fields. Wholly delightful.

Price	£85. Singles £52.50.
Rooms	2 twins/doubles.
Meals	Dinner £25. Restaurant 2.5 miles.
Closed	Rarely.
Directions	A46 from Evesham or Stratford; exit for Salford Priors. On entering village, right opp. church, for Dunnington. House on right, approx. 1 mile on, after 2nd sign on right for Dunnington.

Jane & Richard Beach
Salford Farm House, Salford Priors,
Evesham WR11 8XN

Tel	01386 870000
Email	salfordfarmhouse@aol.com
Web	www.salfordfarmhouse.co.uk

Entry 95   Map 3

Blackwell Grange

The garden: A former rickyard for the farm has been worked into a quarter acre of pretty English garden around the farmhouse. Old York stones with curved raised beds form grand steps up to the lawn; apple trees pop up through hedges; ancient ivy creeps into the thatch; uninvited wild strawberries have been allowed to stay. There's a relaxed feel to all the planting – no strict colour schemes or design-led rigidity – so that the rhythm from garden to countryside is fluent and charming. Perfectly clipped hedges, neat lawns and careful planting around arches and pergolas show a more restrained side to the garden but somehow it all looks effortless anyway. Ancient barns have been used as scaffolding for the old roses, hops, jasmine and clematis which give colour on different levels, and a dear little summerhouse has splendid views over hills and woods. A circular stone seat hides behind a narrow walkway between the barns with more roses and clematis growing over it and hostas sit contentedly in old pots. A productive fruit and vegetable garden is neatly hidden behind the house; Liz's hens roam here, checking for insects and laying breakfast eggs. Lamb is reared too; if you want to take a whole one back for your freezer, just say the word.

The house: Mellow stone, clipped hedges, broad paths, billowing plants and many varieties of hosta. Inside: flagstones, beams, creaking floorboards and a big inglenook. The sitting room comes with old books and worn sofas, and bedrooms with zip-and-link beds; the traditional bedroom upstairs has floral drapes and sheep-dotted views through stone mullion windows. The ground-floor bedroom is set up for wheelchair users and overlooks the garden. There's homemade marmalade and damson jam for breakfast, and eggs from the Lavender Pekin bantams that strut outside.

Price	From £75. Singles from £45.
Rooms	2 twins/doubles.
Meals	Pubs 1-1.5 miles.
Closed	Christmas Day & occasionally.
Directions	From Stratford-upon-Avon, A3400 for Oxford. After 5 miles, right by church in Newbold-on-Stour & follow signs to Blackwell. Fork right on entering Blackwell. Entrance beyond thatched barn.

 Travel Club Offer. See page 290.

Liz Vernon Miller
Blackwell Grange, Blackwell,
Shipston-on-Stour CV36 4PF

Tel	01608 682357
Fax	01608 682856
Email	sawdays@blackwellgrange.co.uk
Web	www.blackwellgrange.co.uk

Entry 96   Map 3

St James's Grange

The garden: A thoroughly pleasing mix of garden influences here: French and English-cottage, and a touch of Elizabethan formality. Carolyn enjoys trying out new ideas as the garden evolves from the field they started with. David has made a grand job of the dry stone walling that borders the terrace (perfect for summer breakfasts) and the small croquet lawn edged with pleached limes (underplanted with chionodoxa and geraniums) and box parterres. There's a thriving walled kitchen garden tucked in by fruit trees and a copse effect of indigenous trees: effectively a windbreak beyond the beech hedging that encircles the sun dial with its lavender surround. The courtyard area to the south of the house is a real sun trap: the raised beds are planted in whites, silvers, pinks, purples and blues echoed by wisteria, honeysuckle, clematis and the pink-flushed 'Phyllis Bide' rambling on the house walls. Terracotta pots at the kitchen door tumble with geraniums and herbs, water gently burbles within a stone urn. It's all so peaceful that partridges nest in the wild garden areas... tiny chicks can sometimes be seen following mum across the lawn. *NGS.*

The house: Next to the church, in a peaceful, pretty South Cotswold hamlet, is a barn conversion; inside it's a serenely comfortable home with good furniture and interesting art finds. Carolyn puts you at ease with tea and homemade cake in the open-fired, French-windowed drawing room. The bright double room has passion-flower curtains framing a garden view; the smaller, minty-fresh double and twin – also with garden views – share a family-style bathroom with a separate shower. This area, celebrated for its lovely market towns also offers excellent walking. Bath and Castle Combe are near. *Children over six welcome.*

Price	£60–£70. Singles from £40.
Rooms	3: 1 twin/double; 1 double, 1 twin sharing bath & shower.
Meals	Pubs 2 miles.
Closed	Christmas & occasionally.
Directions	From A46 for Bath, 2nd left for West Littleton. House on right just after red phone box at top of village green.

Carolyn & David Adams
St James's Grange, West Littleton,
Chippenham SN14 8JE

Tel	01225 891100
Email	dandcadams@stjamesgrange.com
Web	www.stjamesgrange.com

Ridleys Cheer

The garden: Plantsmen traditionally sacrifice design on the altar of collecting, but Antony and Sue combine both in a 14-acre garden packed with roses, wildflowers, rare shrubs and trees. Born gardeners, the Youngs began here modestly 40 years ago. In the lower and upper gardens, lawns sweep through displays including 120 different shrub and species roses, daphnes, tulip trees, a walnut grove and 15 different magnolias. The maturing arboretum contains a wide range of trees – beech, planes, hollies, manna ash, zelkova, 30 different oaks – through which roses cascade; broad mown rides radiate among acers in small glades. Serbian spruce were selected to attract goldcrests, which now nest here. Beyond is a three-acre wildflower meadow with 40 species of native limestone flora, a magnet for butterflies in June and July. By the house are touches of formality in potager and box garden, but the overall mood is of a profuse and breathtaking informality with glorious details and a ravishing collection of plants. Antony, garden lecturer and designer, wears his knowledge with engaging lightness. Students are sent here to learn about horticulture; plants are propagated to buy. Ridleys Cheer opens for the NGS and private groups. Exceptional. *NGS, Good Gardens Guide**.

The house: Rest your head on crisp cotton, wake to garden fruits and home-baked bread: Sue looks after you superbly. The pretty house, in a peaceful hamlet down a meandering lane nine miles from Bath, was once a small cottage. Twenty years ago it was enlarged, one addition being the scented conservatory where you breakfast among oleander, jasmine and plumbago; new too is the spacious drawing room, inviting with log fires and books. Bedrooms, reached by a separate staircase, are light, airy and charming, with enticing garden views. Sue is an experienced Cordon Bleu chef; dinners, served at the mahogany table, are divine.

Price	From £90. Singles £55.
Rooms	3: 1 double; 1 double, 1 twin, sharing bath.
Meals	Lunch £20. Dinner with wine, from £35. Pub 2 miles.
Closed	Occasionally.
Directions	M4 junc. 17. At Chippenham, A420 for Bristol; 9 miles, right at x-roads in hamlet, The Shoe; 2nd left; 1st right into Mountain Bower (no sign). Last house on left; park on drive opposite.

Sue & Antony Young
Ridleys Cheer, Mountain Bower,
Chippenham SN14 7AJ

Tel	01225 891204
Fax	01225 891139
Email	sueyoung@ridleyscheer.co.uk
Web	www.ridleyscheer.co.uk

Travel Club Offer. See page 290.

Ethical Collection: Food.
See page 294.

Great Chalfield Manor

The garden: Stand in the middle of the lawn, close your eyes and imagine that Titania and Oberon have just fluttered past – open your eyes and they have. A structure of neatly clipped yew houses, upper and lower moats, herbaceous borders, huge lawns and an orchard have been immaculately tended and then enchanced by Patsy's love of soft colour and roses. The south-facing rose terrace brims over with scented pink roses that bloom all summer long, ramblers scrabble over anything with height, including old stone walls and the fruit trees in the orchard – and they are not alone; there is honeysuckle in abundance too, rambling hither and thither to waft its gorgeous English smell. Lavender and nepeta – the gentlest of hues – even the 'red border' is soft with smudgy colour, never garish. Water weaves through the grass in little streams which feed the serene, lily-laden moats and there is a magical woodland walk bursting with snowdrops in February. Patsy learned about gardening by "doing it" and gains ideas and inspiration from the tours she organises for 'The Garden Party' – but she has very firm ideas of her own especially when it comes to design and colour. There is a hazy, bloom-filled dreaminess about Great Chalfield. Perhaps Puck really does sprinkle something into your eyes as you go up the long, grassy drive... *NGS, Good Gardens Guide.*

The house: A National Trust house – a rare example of the English medieval manor complete with 14th-century church and a family home where you will be treated as a guest not a visitor. Flagstones, a Great Hall with Flemish tapestries, perfect panelling, fine oak furniture and ancient elegance inspire awe – but Patsy dispels all formality with a gorgeous smile. Proper four-posters in the stone-walled bedrooms are swathed in the softest greens and pinks, the bathrooms are deeply old-fashioned and the only sound is bird ballad. Kitchen suppers follow large drinks in the prettiest panelled sitting room. *Special two-night stays with local gardens tour.*

Price	From £100. Singles from £80.
Rooms	2 four-posters, each with separate bath.
Meals	Supper £25. Pub/restaurant 1 mile.
Closed	Occasionally.
Directions	From Melksham B3107 for Bradford on Avon. 1st right to Broughton Gifford, through village, first left signed Great Chalfield, 1 mile drive.

Patsy Floyd
Great Chalfield Manor,
Melksham SN12 8NH
Tel   01225 782239
Email   patsy@greatchalfield.co.uk

Ethical Collection: Environment;
Community; Food. See page 294.

Entry 99   Map 3

Broomsgrove Lodge

The garden: Some people just seem to have the knack for creating inviting surroundings outside as well as in. Diana moved to Broomsgrove Lodge in 1996 after six months in Hong Kong, and is happily occupied tending home, guests and garden. The Robertsons found themselves a picture-book setting: the thatched house gazes over serene and open countryside, and the (wonderfully comfortable) conservatory they added makes the most of the views. From the slope outside a sunken terrace was created: a mass of pots planted with colourful annuals and bulbs, all grown on site. The pots continue up the steps leading onto an exceptionally well-groomed lawn – not a daisy in sight. The grandchildren love the camomile seat cut into the terrace retaining wall, and the lovers' seat that encircles the trunk of the oak tree higher up, a charming spot from which to gaze on the gravel garden and herbaceous border. Summer's sweetpeas are spectacular and fill the house with scent. But Diana's greatest pleasure is the vegetable garden groaning with produce, much of which goes to family and friends.

The house: Here is a pretty thatched house with an owner who has a talent for both gardening and interior design. The sitting room, decorated in terracotta and pale green, leads to a lovely big conservatory with fine views of garden and hills. Diana serves breakfast here or in the farmhouse kitchen: eggs from the hens that strut in the field, and – rare treat – freshly squeezed orange juice. There are fresh, pretty bedrooms (TV-free) with polished bathrooms, beautiful furniture and pictures bought back from Hong Kong. Lots to do during the day and the Avon & Kennet Canal tow path a step away.

Price	From £75. Singles £40.
Rooms	3: 1 twin; 1 twin with separate bath; 1 extra single available.
Meals	Pub/restaurant 1.5 miles.
Closed	Christmas & New Year.
Directions	From Hungerford A338 Burbage r'bout B3087 to Pewsey. Right in Milton Lilbourne to New Mill; under bridge, through village, over canal; lodge on left at entrance to farm.

Mrs Peter Robertson
Broomsgrove Lodge,
New Mill, Pewsey SN9 5LE

Tel	01672 810515
Email	diana@broomsgrovelodge.co.uk

The Mill House

The garden: The feel of family heritage in this house is perhaps most at evidence in the garden, which looms large within the passions of both Michael and Diana. Diana's love of gardening came from her mother, who taught her everything she knows. The whole garden spreads its rambling self over more than 12 acres, in which four 'rooms' predominate. Despite such a structure, wildlife and songbirds are the valued inhabitants of this alfresco extravaganza, who exist in and around the 200 species of roses, the old wooden summer house and the (weather dependent) water-filled ditch that divides the garden. Many of the apples, pears and tomatoes that will catch your eye find their way onto the breakfast table. The chalk stream flanking the garden harbours a Site of Special Scientific Interest and those in the know will instantly recognise the preconditions of a haven for butterflies and other environment rewarding species; the marsh orchids are a glory in May and June. The love of the owners for their own 'Garden of Eden' will no doubt enthuse any who cross the wide wooden bridge at its opening. If a garden can be a day's entertainment, then a couple of weeks may be required for this one. *NGS.*

The house: In a tranquil village next to the river is a house surrounded by water meadows and wilderness garden. Roses ramble, marsh orchids bloom and butterflies shimmer. This 12-acre labour of love is the creation of Diana, now in her 80s, and her son Michael. Their home, the time-worn 18th-century miller's house, is packed with country clutter – porcelain, teddy bears, ancestral photographs above the fire – while bedrooms are quaint, old-fashioned and flowery, with firm, comfy beds. The family has lived here over 46 years and has been doing B&B for 26 of them.

Price	From £85. Singles from £55.
Rooms	5: 3 doubles, 1 family room; 1 twin with separate bath.
Meals	Pub 5-minute walk.
Closed	Never.
Directions	From A303 B3083 at Winterbourne Stoke to Berwick St James. Go through village, past Boot Inn & church. Turn left into yard just before the sharp left bend. Coming from A36 (B3083), house 1st on right.

Diana Gifford Mead & Michael Mertens
The Mill House,
Berwick St James, Salisbury SP3 4TS

Tel	01722 790331
Fax	01722 790753
Web	www.millhouse.org.uk

Old Stoke

The garden: When Tracie arrived at her new home, just over 12 years ago, she found a one-and-a-half acre field around the house, so she started her garden from scratch. She very much wanted it to complement the house so, with a picture-perfect thatched cottage, she has created a gentle garden, reassuringly traditional and highly scented. Old roses and peonies tumble in deep herbaceous borders flanking a smooth croquet lawn. From here you can walk down an avenue of evergreen oak, prunus, acers, rowan, ash and silver birch, to the flowing chalk stream and the green meadows. A hedge grows silently taller to mask a 'secret' garden with iris, roses, old apple trees and a mulberry. Forget-me-nots and foxgloves are self-seeding merrily in the country cottage garden, which is divided by a trellis from the lawn. All the paths and patios have been laid by Tracie and Matthew, who seem to do most things from scratch: growing from seed, taking cuttings, dividing plants are a favourite hobby and they are generous with guests. There are plenty of spots to sit and have a cup of tea or glass of wine, and a super veg patch to visit – most of what you see will end up on your plate. Delicious.

The house: As pretty as thatched cottages come. This lovely old farmhouse is edged by an AONB filled with birdsong and wildlife, yet you are close to Salisbury. Guests have a book-filled sitting room with Dorset cream walls and pretty chairs and sofas to collapse onto: upstairs are fresh bedrooms with bright fabrics on headboards and window cushions, feathery beds and sparkling bathrooms. Tracie is charming and cooks well; good wholesome food using eggs from her own hens, vegetables from the garden and delicious flapjacks or cake for tea. Lovely walking straight from the door.

Price	£60-£65. Singles £35-£40.
Rooms	2: 1 twin/double; 1 double with separate bath.
Meals	Dinner £15-£20. Packed lunch £6. Pub 1 mile.
Closed	December-February.
Directions	SW from Salisbury on A354; right at Coombe Bissett dir. Bishopstone. 2nd left after White Hart, signed Stoke Farthing. In hamlet, sharp bend to right, 2nd house on left. Parking to left of house.

Tracie Pickford
Old Stoke, Stoke Farthing,
Broadchalke, Salisbury SP5 5ED

Tel	01722 780513
Email	traciepickford@hotmail.co.uk
Web	www.oldstoke.co.uk

Weobley Cross Cottage

The garden: Anne and Peter have clearly poured love, thought and passion into their patch of nearly an acre with stunning views across Herefordshire. In five years they have transformed an overgrown, concrete-infested wilderness into four delightful areas. Between the house and the forge is the suburban garden with its neatly clipped lawn and flowering shrubs in a wide border; a *Magnolia stellata* in a half barrel is stunning in April and there's a glorious deep red smoke bush. New paths from here take you to a gravel patio area, perfect for a drink or breakfast – views are through forsythia, clematis, jasmine and honeysuckle to the pretty cottage garden with its old-fashioned roses, arch rails, grass paths and peaceful pond bustling with dragonflies. In the evening, the lower lawn is the place to be for stunning sunsets among the plum and damson trees; romantics can swing gently in a cushioned seat and watch the clear night sky… you may hear a barn owl too. An abundant kitchen garden area, with greenhouse, will soon be home also to chickens. Work is divided pretty equally: Peter in charge of vegetables, lawns and hedges, Anne in charge of the plants and borders that she adores to fill with colour and scent. A delightful garden which you are free to explore at your own pace.

The house: Come for the wonderful Malvern hills, pasture land dotted with cows and sheep and a pretty Victorian cottage with a neat extension. Inside, tea and biscuits, immaculate bedrooms with floral curtains, cream bedspreads and old pine, and compact sparkling shower rooms with good thick towels. All is incredibly tickety-boo thanks to Peter's building skills and Anne's talent for co-ordinating colours. You breakfast in the conservatory overlooking the garden on local sausages and organic eggs: walk it off in stunning countryside – or head for Malvern with its spring flower show and nearby good nurseries.

Price	From £75.
Rooms	2: 1 double, 1 twin.
Meals	Pub/restaurant 2 miles.
Closed	Christmas.
Directions	From Great Malvern, A449 for Ledbury. Right for Colwell, then right for West Malvern. After 1 mile, left into Harcourt Road. Continue 2 miles towards Mathon. House on left at head of South End Lane.

Peter Haywood
Weobley Cross Cottage, South End Lane,
Mathon, Malvern WR13 5PB

Tel	01684 541488
Email	anne@hanleyinteriors.co.uk
Web	www.bedandbreakfastmalvernhills.co.uk

Travel Club Offer. See page 290.

Entry 103   Map 2

Millgate House

The garden: Nothing about the elegant façade of Austin and Tim's home hints at the treasures which lie behind. Wandering into the drawing room you are drawn, magnet-like, to the veranda to discover the full impact of the garden below. A stay at Millgate House without exploring it would be an unforgivable omission; no wonder that when Austin and Tim entered the Royal Horticultural Society's 1995 National Garden Competition they romped away with first prize. This famous walled town garden deserves every last bouquet and adulatory article it has received. A narrow shady lane to one side of the house, adorned with immaculate hostas, introduces the main garden. Here the long terraced grounds, sloping steeply down towards the river and overlooked by the great Norman castle, are divided into a rhythmic series of lush compartments. All is green, with cascades of foliage breaking out into small, sunny open areas before you dive beneath yet more foliage to explore further secret areas. Plantsmanship, a passion for old roses, hostas, clematis, ferns and small trees and a love of many different leaf forms come together triumphantly. As William Blake said: "Exuberance is beauty". If you just want to explore the garden you can phone Austin and Tim to arrange a visit. *NGS, Good Gardens Guide, RHS Associate Garden.*

The house: Prepare to be amazed. In every room of the house and in every corner of the garden, the marriage of natural beauty and sophistication exists in a state of bliss. The four Doric columns at the entrance draw you through the hall into the dining room and to views of the Swale Valley. Beds from Heals, period furniture, cast-iron baths, myriad prints and paintings and one double bed so high you wonder how to get onto it. Tim and Austin, both ex-English teachers, have created something special, and breakfasts are superb.

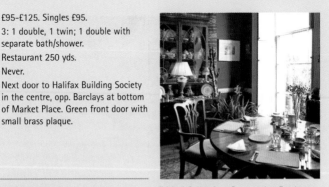

Price	£95–£125. Singles £95.
Rooms	3: 1 double, 1 twin; 1 double with separate bath/shower.
Meals	Restaurant 250 yds.
Closed	Never.
Directions	Next door to Halifax Building Society in the centre, opp. Barclays at bottom of Market Place. Green front door with small brass plaque.

Austin Lynch & Tim Culkin
Millgate House,
Richmond DL10 4JN

Tel	01748 823571
Fax	01748 850701
Email	oztim@millgatehouse.demon.co.uk
Web	www.millgatehouse.com

Ethical Collection: Community; Food.
See page 294.

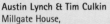

Cold Cotes

The garden: What was a five-acre field, facing a dominant westerly, has been shaken up royally! It is now a series of dazzling 'zones' starting next to the house with a stone-flagged terrace with clumps of thrift, miniature geraniums, euphorbias and pots of blue agapanthus. In front is a red bed made up of oriental poppies, dahlias, tulips and penstemon, then stone steps down to a formal garden. Golden hops scrabble over an obelisk, a pond is surrounded by sunny herb beds and hedging breaks it up into sections. Another hot bed is around the corner, a woodland walk is planted with cherry, sorbus, beech, alders and oak and there are some impressive sweeping borders inspired by the designer Piet Oudolf and containing his beloved prairie plants and grasses. A cobblestone walk (Penny Lane) ambles along a stream with a little bridge, planted around with gunnera, periwinkle, ivy and comfrey, leading to a thriving pond. A fruit and veg garden provides abundant produce; a little lawned area is surrounded by cherry trees and has a perfect seating area with old wooden furniture. A new garden focusing on shade lovers in a woodland setting is in its first exciting season; a circular wooded walk with naturalistic planting is in preparation. A garden for quiet contemplation, filled with birdsong. *Open to the public first Sunday in September & by appointment.*

The house: Ed and Penny have meticulously restored this 1890s farmhouse on the edge of the Yorkshire Dales. A sitting room with polished boards, creamy walls, squashy sofas, roaring fire and loads of books is covered in Ed's paintings (his studio is upstairs). The light, long dining room with its three full-length windows faces the garden and has a sprung floor should you need to dance. Bedrooms are purpose-designed for B&B with pale walls and carpets, brass beds, fine thick fabrics, roomy bathrooms and some long garden views. Homemade cakes for tea, local bacon and sausages for breakfast, local and home-grown produce for evening meals.

Price	From £80.
Rooms	6: 4 doubles, 2 twins/doubles (2 with own sitting rooms).
Meals	Light bites & supper by arrangement. Pub/restaurant 2.5 miles.
Closed	2 weeks in January.
Directions	A59 from Harrogate for 7 miles towards Skipton. Right after Black Bull pub, signed RAF Menwith, onto Cold Cotes Road. Third on right, 500 yards from A59.

Ed Loft
Cold Cotes, Felliscliffe,
Harrogate HG3 2LW

Tel	01423 770937
Email	info@coldcotes.com
Web	www.coldcotes.com

Travel Club Offer. See page 290.

Entry 105   Map 6

Fountains House

The garden: An old lady used to live here and the garden had become horribly overgrown; ivy rampaged and sombre firs blotted out the wide country views. When Clive and Gill took over in 2004, they sacrificed all but one of the firs but kept the two large Corsican pines (the cones make fabulous firelighters). Clearing the choked herbaceous borders, they planted foxgloves, delphiniums and roses among the shrubs, with exochorda and variegated philadelphus peeping out from the jumbled, cottage-garden mix. It's pretty and unpretentious: a smooth lawn for croquet; roses on the walls; a hidden dell with a bench for a quiet read; almond and cherry trees, lilac and laburnum. The country-cottage feel is enhanced by a generous scattering of honeysuckle, lilies and peonies, and there's a sweet herb garden by the front door. Beyond an old low stone wall, an expanse of cornfield stretches into the distance. Unsurprisingly, pheasants and partridge are frequent visitors, as well as blackbirds and thrushes, wrens and wagtails. Altogether an interesting and charming garden – and the parasoled terrace makes a delightful spot for tea.

The house: Warm stone under a terracotta roof: Fountains is a house full of sunshine on the edge of the village. Fat sofas and charmingly grouped pictures make the elegant sitting room an inviting spot to spend an evening, while the fresh, pretty bedrooms promise a good sleep (in spite of a little road noise in the room at the front). The twin has a garden view, the bathrooms are lovely. Your hosts, friendly and hospitable without being intrusive, give you fresh fruit, homemade bread and a piping hot fry-up at breakfast, and if you become addicted to Gill's wonderful jams and marmalades, you can buy a jar to take home.

Price	£72-£80.
Rooms	2: 1 double, 1 twin.
Meals	Pubs 3-minute walk.
Closed	Rarely.
Directions	From A61 Harrogate Ripon road, turning for Burton Leonard at garage. Enter village, house on right, 500 yds. From A1 exit at junc. 48. Signed for Burton Leonard. Through village, past green, house 200 yds on left.

Clive & Gill King
Fountains House, Burton Leonard,
Harrogate HG3 3RU

Tel	01765 677537
Email	info@fountainshouse.co.uk
Web	www.fountainshouse.co.uk

Shallowdale House

The garden: Keep climbing and by the time you get to the top of these two very lush acres you will feel you've had a country hike... so perch on a bench and drink in the Yorkshire air. The many specimen trees planted when the house was built 40-odd years ago are growing up beautifully. Weeping birch, cypress, cherry, maple, acer and copper beech hover over swathes of grass underplanted with thousands of bulbs, a double rockery groans with scented shrubs like viburnum, rosemary and choisya; cistus, hardy geraniums, ceanothus, fuchsias and potentilla are popped in for colour. Lose yourself in the landscape – a lovely park-like atmosphere prevails – and sit and soak up the peace. Nearer the house there are more formal beds, a mini-orchard, a sunny terrace with tinkling water and clematis and roses that romp over the arches... mixed planting everywhere but in such good taste. Much discussion is of future projects and what to tackle next; hard work for just the two of them but Anton never goes up, or down, the hill without an armful of dead-heads and flotsam. Come for views which sweep from the Pennines to the Wolds.

The house: Phillip and Anton have a true affection for their guests so you will be treated like angels in small-hotel style. Sumptuous bedrooms dazzle in yellows, blues and limes, acres of curtains frame wide views over the Howardian Hills, bathrooms are gleaming. Breakfast on the absolute best; fresh fruit compote, dry-cured bacon, homemade rolls – and walk it off in any direction from the door. Return to an elegant drawing room, with a fire in winter, and an enticing library. Dinner is out of this world and coffee and chocolates are all you need before you crawl up to bed. Bliss. *Minimum stay two nights at weekends.*

Price	£95-£115. Singles £75-£85.
Rooms	3: 2 twins/doubles; 1 double with separate bath/shower.
Meals	Dinner, 4 courses, £35.
Closed	Christmas & New Year.
Directions	From Thirsk, A19 south, then 'caravan route' via Coxwold & Byland Abbey. 1st house on left, just before Ampleforth.

Anton van der Horst & Phillip Gill
Shallowdale House,
West End, Ampleforth YO62 4DY

Tel	01439 788325
Fax	01439 788885
Email	stay@shallowdalehouse.co.uk
Web	www.shallowdalehouse.co.uk

Ethical Collection: Food.
See page 294.

Riverside Farm

The garden: Not only have Jane and Bill created a beautiful two-acre garden by the river, but Jane is the National Gardens Scheme organiser for North Yorkshire. Her knowledge of every garden and owner on her patch means she can arrange private visits – and there is much to relish here, too. As you open the little gate that leads to the front door, two old stone troughs overflowing with helichrysum and geraniums introduce you to a dream of a cottage garden. Inspired by Rosemary Verey's circular lawn with four beds at Barnsley, Jane keeps a close eye on the colours, preferring to keep pink plants to a minimum, and has a light touch when controlling the self-seeding. The overall effect is beautifully natural and uncontrived – not easy, as any gardener will tell you. Pretty pink shrub roses have been given special permission to romp in the long, deep herbaceous bed that is, again, artfully natural. This runs parallel to the river that flows down the garden's eastern border. A 'Kiftsgate' rose amply covers a 30-foot barn, and from the garden behind, through the huge rose arch of 'Félicite et Perpetue', is a vista that invites you to explore the wild area, lovely with pond and mown paths meandering towards new woodland. *NGS.*

The house: A charming long, low Georgian farmhouse that overlooks the river and the village green. Gleaming old family furniture, Bill's family photographs up the stairs, and two handsome bedrooms facing south over the cottage garden. There's Colefax & Fowler sweet pea wallpaper in the twin, and Osborne & Little topiary trees in its bathroom. Breakfast is deliciously traditional – this is a working farm – and there's a lovely guest sitting room to come home to. Elegant surroundings, excellent value and Jane a practical and generous hostess who looks after you well. Special indeed. *Minimum stay two nights.*

Price	From £65. Singles £40.
Rooms	3: 1 double; 1 twin with separate bath; 1 single with separate or shared bath.
Meals	Pub/restaurant 5-minute walk.
Closed	November-March.
Directions	From Pickering A170; 4 miles to Sinnington. Into village, cross river; right into lane for Riverside Farm.

Bill & Jane Baldwin
Riverside Farm, Sinnington,
Pickering YO62 6RY

Tel	01751 431764
Fax	01751 431764
Email	wnbaldwin@yahoo.co.uk

Wales

Broniwan

The garden: Carole and Allen's committment to the environment and passionate interest in wildlife are what makes this garden special, and a Tir Gofal Educational Access farm surrounds it. Carole designed the formal parts around the house, extending and replanting the original beds. There's a small lawned area on the upper level bordered by deep beds of hydrangea, aquilegia, agapanthus and rosemary with a little wrought-iron fence covered in clematis at the front. The narrow pathways, built with bricks from an old pig-sty and with Victorian tiled edging, lead to a large shrub border of camellias and rhododendrons, bamboo, ceanothus, irises, broom and bright pieris; then more lawns and a rose bed. Further on is a border of eucalyptus trees and the fruit and vegetable garden. A mown path through the grasses meanders to the meadow; meticulous records are kept of all the animals, birds, wildflowers and trees. Broadleaf woodlands, waterside and wetland areas, hedgerow restoration and maintenance, parkland, pond areas and grassland meadows mean Broniwan is teeming with birds (including the elusive red kite), butterflies, rare wildflowers and even otters. Allen is happy to take guests on farm walks; Carole loves the garden and will chat easily about her plans.

The house: Carole and Allen have created a model organic farm, and it shows. They are happy, the cows are happy and the kitchen garden is the neatest in Wales. With huge warmth and a tray of Welsh cakes they invite you into their ivy-clad home, cosy and inviting with its warm natural colours and the odd vibrant flourish of local art. Another passion is literature (call to arrange a literary weekend). Tree-creepers, wrens and redstarts nest in the garden, there are views to the Preseli hills, the National Botanic Garden of Wales and Aberglasney are nearby, and the unspoilt coast is a ten-minute drive.

Price	£65-£70. Singles £35.
Rooms	2: 1 double; 1 double with separate bath.
Meals	Dinner £25-£30. BYO. Restaurant 7-8 miles.
Closed	Rarely.
Directions	From Aberaeron, A487 for 6 miles for Brynhoffnant. Left at B4334 to Rhydlewis; left at Post Office & shop, 1st lane on right, then 1st track on right.

Carole & Allen Jacobs
Broniwan,
Rhydlewis, Llandysul SA44 5PF

Tel	01239 851261
Fax	01239 851261
Email	broniwan@btinternet.com
Web	www.broniwan.com

Rhydlewis House

The garden: Judith can look out on her acre of garden with pride: the planting, apart from a few mature trees and some crocosmia, is entirely her own. There are several seats from which to admire the fruits of Judith's labours, and the garden, begun in the spring of 2000, has matured well. The upper level of two main areas of lawn has an arbour tucked into an angle of the old workshop building, from where you can gaze back up at the house. On the lower lawn white-flowering shrubs form a backdrop against a wall to the gravel garden; rest on a bench and admire the hot reds, oranges and yellows of crocosmia in the herbaceous border opposite. Walk through the honeysuckle arch and discover a wide mixture of flowering shrubs: evergreens (protection from the wind), weigela, berberis and hydrangeas for season-long colour, and an under-planting of primroses, violets and *Anemone blanda*. From yet another seat you can watch all the village comings and goings. No modern garden is complete without a deck and Judith's makes an ideal spot for tea or an evening drink; as you sip, admire her pots of hostas, fuchsias and begonias.

The house: An 18th-century house in a friendly village with a wealth of nurseries – perfect for gardeners. This ex-drovers' trading post mixes traditional with new: modern furniture by students of John Makepeace, exposed stone walls, rugs on polished wooden floors. The dining room has quarry tiles, an inglenook and Welsh oak cottage-style chairs. A sunny double room with gold curtains overlooks the garden; warm reds, oranges and creams are the colours of the twin. Judith is a terrific cook who uses mostly local produce (Welsh cheeses, an excellent smokery in the village). Single visitors are particularly welcome.

Price	£56-£60. Singles £28-£30.
Rooms	3: 1 double, 1 twin; 1 double with separate bath.
Meals	Dinner £20. BYO. Restaurant 5 miles.
Closed	Christmas.
Directions	North on A487. Right at north side of Sarnau, signed 'Rhydlewis'. T-junc. right to B4334. In Rhydlewis at sharp right bend, left. 40 yards on left.

Judith Russill
Rhydlewis House,
Rhydlewis, Llandysul SA44 5PE

Tel	01239 851748
Email	judithrussill@aol.com
Web	www.rhydlewis-house.co.uk

The Yat

The garden: In a supreme setting of rolling hills studded with sheep is the Yat: a listed house dating from the 15th century, with logs piled in the porch and swallows dipping in and out. The sloping terraces around the house are thought to date from Elizabethan times; the remains of flagstone paths can be detected still. Years ago Krystyna and Derek fell in love with these eight acres, where nature predominates and the only sounds you hear are birdsong and whispering wind. The first thing they did was plant trees on the steep slopes to the sides. Now there are 1,000 — mostly deciduous, some coniferous — providing shelter for plants and a wonderful haven for wildlife. The ancient terraces were extended in the south-facing part of the garden, retained by ivy-straggled stone walls and reached by stone steps. The garden, an on-going project, is a mixture of formal and wild: of blackcurrant bushes and wild strawberry plants that have merrily self-seeded, of tiered organic vegetable gardens and topiary. Pass the overgrown pond down the lane to the ruins of a baptistry and a tiny patch of burial ground. Or sit by the fountain that trickles over the little cast-iron boy with swans, and hear the doves coo. There's a sense of timelessness to this place: in Krystyna's words, "a unity of mind, man and nature".

The house: Come for stunning scenery, a characterful household and an engaging hostess. The listed house, once the home of the wicked squire of Bevan, has hung on to its ancient flags and beams; the feel, thanks to charming artist Krystyna, is one of calm, and there are many beautiful things to look at. Bedrooms are quaint, bathrooms plain with special touches (white robes, good soaps) and there's space to roam: a sitting room, a conservatory, a snug library with games. Food is almost all organic, breakfasts and suppers scrumptious and local. This is a grand place to really rest and recharge your batteries.

Price	£75. Singles from £55.
Rooms	2: 1 double, 1 twin.
Meals	Dinner, 3 courses, £30 (incl. glass of wine, coffee & biscuits).
Closed	Rarely.
Directions	Directions from Hundred House village: road to Glascwm, signed at crossroads; at next T-junc., left over hump-backed bridge; left at next junction; 1st house on right.

Krystyna Zaremba
The Yat, Glascwm,
Llandrindod Wells LD1 5SE

Tel	01982 570339
Fax	01982 551032
Email	krystyna.zaremba@theyat.net
Web	www.theyat.net

Travel Club Offer. See page 290.

Ethical Collection: Environment; Food.
See page 294.

Entry 111   Map 2

Allt-y-bela

The garden: There is a magical garden being created here by the owner, Chelsea Gold Medal winner Arne Maynard, with formal topiary, dramatic earth sculpture and gentle native planting. The garden melts into the landscape around the house with no boundaries at all, so that in this intensely private place, nature meets nurture with a sense of wonder that is very special indeed. In the spring there are massed snowdrops and wild narcissus which give way to carpets of primroses and bluebells. Blossom abounds in pleached fruit trees and all through the hedgerows. Summer brings wild orchids to the fields around the house and innumerable other rare and beautiful wildflowers. There is a productive organic kitchen garden yielding lovingly cared-for vegetables bursting with flavour, picked only just before being prepared for the table. Arne runs an acclaimed series of gardening courses from here with seminars and demonstrations throughout the year using his garden as a backdrop. Visitors are able to relax here all day or walk and explore this beautiful and secret valley with its streams, coppiced woods, pastures and drove-ways.

The house: A beautiful and ancient house, built between 1420 and 1599, kicking off an early Renaissance architectural buzz and now perfectly restored for the 21st century. It is reached down a narrow lane in its own private and secluded valley. Here is made-to-measure pampering among soaring beams and period furniture. A log-warmed dining room for private meals delivered by two clever chefs, and a big farmhouse kitchen if you want to be more involved. Bedrooms soothe with limewashed walls, fabulous beds, no TV, stunning art, and proper bathrooms. A wonderful retreat that you won't forget.

Price	£125.
Rooms	2 doubles.
Meals	Farmhouse supper £30.
	Any other meals by arrangement.
	Pubs/restaurants 3 miles.
Closed	Rarely.
Directions	A449 for Usk, then B4235 to Chepstow.
	After 200 yds, unsigned right turn.
	Follow for 0.5 miles; left into 'No
	Through Road', follow for 0.5 miles.

William Collinson & Arne Maynard
Allt-y-bela,
Llangwm Ucha, Usk NP15 1EZ

Mobile	07892 403103
Email	bb@alltybela.co.uk
Web	www.alltybela.co.uk

Scotland

Newtonmill House

The garden: Stephen and Rose have been enlarging and enhancing these lovely gardens for 24 years. Borders, beds, lawns, woodland and pastures are bounded by old walls, hedges and burns. At the heart of it all is the walled garden that faces the gracious laird's house, its 'entrance' an iron gate in the shape of a mill wheel, its grass walk bounded by herbaceous borders. Formal box hedges edge rectangular beds where fruit, vegetables and flowers grow in glorious profusion — one full of irises, another of peonies. Another contains a croquet lawn, perfect with a revolving summer house and an arbour of honeysuckle and clematis. Espaliered and fan-trained apples, pears and plums clothe the walls, roses clamber and fall in a delicious harmony of scents and hues, a group of Japanese maples shades *Podophyllum hexandrum* and, in a corner, an 18th-century 'doocot' stands, home to happy doves. The heavy soil has been improved over the years with horse and sheep manure; most of the crops are grown with organic principles in mind, and much surplus is given away. Twenty varieties of potato are grown, the raspberries do famously and, in the woodland areas, primroses, bluebells, narcissi and martagon lilies thrive.

The house: The house and grounds are in apple-pie order; the owners are charming and unobtrusive. This is a little-known part of Scotland; come to explore the glens, find deserted beaches and traditional fishing villages, or play a round or two of golf on one of the many good courses nearby. Return to a cup of tea in the elegant sitting room, then a proper supper of seasonal, local and homegrown produce. Later find crisp sheets, soft blankets, feather pillows, fresh flowers, homemade fruit cake and sparkling, warm bathrooms with thick towels; you will be deeply comfortable here. *Children over ten welcome.*

Price	£96–£110. Singles from £60.
Rooms	2: 1 twin; 1 double with separate bath.
Meals	Dinner, 4 courses, from £28.
	Supper, 2 courses, from £18. BYO.
	Packed lunch £10. Pub 3 miles.
Closed	Christmas.
Directions	Aberdeen-Dundee A90, turning
	marked Brechin/Edzell B966. Heading
	towards Edzell, Newtonmill House is
	1 mile on left, drive marked by pillars
	and sign.

Rose & Stephen Rickman
Newtonmill House,
Brechin DD9 7PZ

Tel	01356 622533
Email	rrickman@srickman.co.uk
Web	www.newtonmillhouse.co.uk

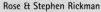 Travel Club Offer. See page 290.

Ethie Castle

The garden: Adrian and Kirstin started this garden from scratch two years ago: they have planted for structure, colour and diversity, and with the primary aim of increasing the bird, butterfly and bee population. There are six acres of formal gardens around the house including a walled vegetable garden, a parterre criss-crossed with box hedging, herbaceous borders and a rose garden. Wander across smooth lawns, admire the new fountain and the old folly (1910), visit the glasshouses brimming with ancient vines. Planting is in long-lasting coloured swathes, and especially hardy varieties have been chosen to cope with sea air, wind and cooler temperatures. Twelve hundred mixed hardwood trees have been planted, there is a restored lime avenue, beech hedging and yew walks. The vegetable garden positively bursts: with beans, sweetcorn, chard, three types of potatoes, Jerusalem artichokes, salads, horseradish and soft fruit – raspberries, gooseberries, blackcurrants, redcurrants – all for the table. There's a lovely summer house for an evening cup of tea or something stronger, and plenty of wildlife to watch; toads, frogs, deer and hares, and birds including tree creepers and siskins. A garden to visit time and time again.

The house: Amazing: a listed Peel tower that dates from 1300 and which once was home to the Abbot of Arbroath, murdered in St Andrews on Henry VIII's orders. His private chapel remains, as does his secret stair. As for the rest of the house: turret staircases, a green Art Deco bathroom, a 1500s ceiling in the Great Hall, a Tudor kitchen with a walk-in fireplace that burns night and day. Kirstin and Adrian are experts at breathing new life into old houses; all is done with supreme elegance and unpushy flair. Lunan Bay, one of Scotland's most beautiful beaches, is at the end of the road. There's a loch too.

Price	From £95. Singles from £75.
Rooms	3: 1 four-poster; 1 twin/double, 1 double, each with separate bath/shower.
Meals	Dinner, 4 courses with wine, £30. Packed lunch up to £10. Pub/restaurant 3 miles.
Closed	Rarely.
Directions	North from Arbroath on A92; right after Shell garage for Auchmithie; left at T-junc.; on for 2 miles; at phone box, private road to Ethie Barns in front.

Adrian & Kirstin de Morgan
Ethie Castle, Inverkeilor,
Arbroath DD11 5SP

Tel	01241 830434
Fax	01241 830432
Email	kmydemorgan@aol.com
Web	www.ethiecastle.com

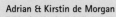

Achamore House

The garden: Don is probably the luckiest gardener in the world: the Isle of Gigha Trust own and have responsibility for these 52 acres, Don just gets to live in the middle of it all and, in his greenhouse, grow the tropical orchids that are his love – some of the orchids are used to make flower essences which Don sells. Visitors to the house can wander at will through mature woodland, stroll the walled garden, visit the pond garden and, in July and August, have home-baked cakes and tea in the tea tent: there's a huge variety of specimen plants, shrubs, some rare trees and roses. Established in 1944 by Sir James Horlick, then owner of the island, the garden is most famous for rhododendrons, camellias and azaleas – the 'Horlick Collection' has gained international recognition among horticulturalists, but it was becoming neglected. Now the Trust have raised a sum of money for restoration work to start: over the next three years they will be replacing the drainage systems, rebuilding the shelter belt, replacing paths and greenhouses and restocking the gardens; locals call this place the 'jewel in the crown' of Gigha and it's easy to see why. Lovely views, abundant wildlife, a stunning plant collection. Well worth a visit.

The house: No traffic jams here, tucked between the mainland and Islay. Despite its grandeur – turrets, Arts & Crafts doors, plasterwork ceilings – Achamore is not stuffy and neither are Don and Emma, your hosts. A coastal skipper, he can take you to sea, or over to other islands in his Redbay RIB. Find warm wood panelling and light-washed rooms, huge bedrooms with shuttered windows, oversize beds, heavy antiques; all have iPods and music. You get the run of the house – billiard room, library, large lounge, TV room (great for kids). With 50 acres of gardens and a quiet beach it's ideal for big parties or gatherings.

Price	£90–£130. Singles from £35.
Rooms	9: 2 doubles, 1 family room; 2 doubles sharing bath; 2 twins/doubles sharing bath; 2 singles sharing bath.
Meals	Pub/restaurant 1 mile.
Closed	Rarely.
Directions	Uphill from ferry landing, turn left at T-junc.; 1 mile, stone gates on right, signed; house at top of drive.

Don Dennis & Emma Rennie
Achamore House,
Isle of Gigha PA41 7AD

Tel	01583 505400
Fax	01583 505 387
Email	gigha@atlas.co.uk
Web	www.achamorehouse.com

 Travel Club Offer. See page 290.

Entry 115   Map 8

Croys House

The garden: Charming Alan and Patricia – thank goodness for their boundless energy! They inherited this garden about ten years ago: it was neglected and overgrown so took time for them to whip back to shape, but they have kept the original layout. The five-acre plot surrounds the house and includes ancient oak, lime, redwood, beech, chestnut, sycamore and fir – some featured on the Ancient Tree web site; even the topiary is about 50 years old – perfectly crisp yew. To the south of the house is a walled garden with two large Victorian greenhouses; here you will find vegetables, flower borders and soft and hard fruits. Garden architecture buffs will adore the original potting shed and glasshouse boilers – still in position but not functional at the moment. The house is softened by a Virginia creeper which, in autumn, provides a rich and beautiful scarlet cloak; in the centre of the front lawn there is a colchicum bed glowing with pale pink flowers in autumn. Wildflowers and wildlife abound, and in winter certain patches are carpeted with snowdrops, giving way in spring to daffodils, and bluebells in April. This hard-working couple spend as much time as they can in their garden and encourage you to wander through it.

The house: A rather grand house, but very homely too: your ostensibly retired hosts are hard-working farmers who also run a rare-breed meat and wool business. Both are passionate about local produce so you will eat very well indeed – at breakfast and at dinner. The dining room is filled with light from huge Georgian windows, the drawing room is pure country house chic, and the big bedrooms are packed with colour (tartans, polka dots, candy stripes), antiques and good views. One room has a superbly quirky roll top in its bathroom. There's an easy comfort here among lovely people and their family memorabilia.

Price	£70. Singles £40.
Rooms	3: 1 double; 1 four-poster, 1 twin sharing bathroom (let to same party only).
Meals	Dinner £17.50. Pub/restaurant 4 miles.
Closed	Christmas & New Year.
Directions	3.5 miles from Castle Douglas. From town centre, A75 towards Dumfries. After 2.5 miles, left at Corsock sign. 1 mile along this road.

Alan & Patricia Withall
Croys House, Bridge of Urr,
Castle Douglas DG7 3EX

Tel	01556 650237
Fax	01556 650746
Email	alanwithall@aol.com
Web	www.croys-house.co.uk

Entry 116 Map 8

Inwood

The garden: A year after they had finished the house, they started on the garden; it is maturing beautifully, although they modestly confess to having made a few mistakes over the years. Just over an acre was cleared and made ready for 110 tons of top soil, then seeded. Wildlife was a problem so fencing was required: now it has an overcoat of climbing roses and clematis. About 20 large beds are cut into the immaculate lawns and filled with a mixture of structural plants, big shrubs and some unusual foliage. The natural backdrop of woodland provides the inspiration for the hard landscaping; the grass paths swoop, the bog garden boggles, the pond has obediently filled with frogs, toads and newts, the greenhouses are immaculate and an arbour is the place to sit and admire it all. Lindsay takes the planting seriously and hands out monthly leaflets about what is flowering to visitors. There isn't a dull season; tulips in spring, rambling roses in summer, hydrangeas and rare exotics like *Musa basjoo* and *Ensete ventricosum 'Maurelii'* later on. In autumn, colchicums and tricyrtis put in an appearance among the changing leaf tints; in spring, the woodland bursts with snowdrops, wood anemones and trilliums. A real plantsman's garden – and you can buy plants. *SGS, RHS, Good Gardens Guide.*

The house: Lindsay and Irvine built this modern bungalow in 1983 – a 25-minute drive from Princes Street yet embraced by the countryside of the Carberry Tower estate. Supremely comfortable guest rooms have a light, modern feel: beige carpets and laminated floors, waffle weave dressing gowns and snowy white linen, good lighting, cosy chairs by the windows and a garden view. The whole place is as clean as a whistle, you are welcomed with homemade cake and a lovely smile, and the guest sitting room is replete with books and DVDs. And there's a pretty conservatory that opens to the garden – Lindsay's pride and joy.

Price	From £80. Singles from £50.
Rooms	2: 1 double, 1 twin.
Meals	Pub 1 mile.
Closed	Christmas & New Year. Mid-January to mid-March.
Directions	From A1 Edinburgh to Berwick, off at 3rd exit. At traffic lights turn right on A6124 to Dalkeith. Follow signs to Carberry, on A6094; left at Inwood Garden sign.

Lindsay Morrison
Inwood, Carberry,
Musselburgh EH21 8PZ

Tel	0131 665 4550
Email	lindsay@inwoodgarden.com
Web	www.inwoodgarden.com

Travel Club Offer. See page 290.

Ethical Collection: Community.
See page 294.

Entry 117   Map 9

Kirknewton House

The garden: You get the best of two worlds at Kirknewton: a large, comfortable house in peaceful landscaped woodland gardens, and Edinburgh, 30 minutes by car or train. The Welwoods have farmed here since they took over the family home in 1981; both are keen gardeners, and set about maximizing the potential of the garden the moment they arrived. There are azaleas and rhododendrons in brilliant abundance in spring, and primulas and meconopsis scattered throughout. To lengthen the season, a long herbaceous border was created in a walled garden — wonderful in summer. A single long wall remains from an old part of the house that was demolished after the war: it faces south, sheltering the garden from the prevailing wind, and is covered in a glorious array of climbing roses: 'Alchemist', 'Maigold', 'Schoolgirl', 'New Dawn'. A stream flows down by the spring border into a pond in front of the house, where rodgersia and stately gunnera flourish. Fallen estate trees are used to fuel fires in winter. Tinkie is a county organiser for Scotland's Gardens Scheme, so knows all about private gardens in the area — Malleny Garden is close. *SGS.*

The house: A lovely place to stay — charming and old-worldly. Rooms are large, as you'd expect from a house that began in the 17th century. Since the complete reorganisation of the ground floor in the 1980s, many comforts have been added to compliment the history. Expect a fine, polished oak staircase, fresh flowers in the hall and family portraits in gold frames, mix and match towels in traditional bathrooms, an antique four-poster with a garden view. Breakfast is the best of Scottish, and there's lots of fruit too — feast upon it in a stately manner in the dining room, or snug up to the Aga in the kitchen.

Price	£110. Singles £55.
Rooms	2: 1 double, 1 four-poster, each with separate bath.
Meals	Dinner £25. Pub/restaurant 4 miles.
Closed	Christmas-February.
Directions	From either A70 or A71 take B7031. 0.25 miles from Kirknewton going south, drive on left opp. small cottage.

Tinkie & Charles Welwood
Kirknewton House,
Kirknewton EH27 8DA

Tel	01506 881235
Fax	01506 882237
Email	cwelwood@kirknewtonestate.co.uk
Web	www.kirknewtonestate.co.uk

Entry 118 Map 9

Cambo House

The garden: A garden of renown, stunningly romantic all year round. There is a spectacular carpet of snowdrops, snowflakes and aconites in the 70 acres of woodland following the Cambo burn down to the sea; bulbs, including many specialist varieties, are available by mail order. A woodland garden is in a continuing state of development; the lilac walk through 26 varieties is a glorious, sweet-smelling display in May. The Cambo burn carves its way across the two-acre walled garden where a huge range of herbaceous perennials and roses fill the borders with colour. A willow weeps artfully between a decorative bridge and a Chinese-style summerhouse looking as though it has stepped out of a willow-pattern plate. The potager created in 2001 has matured brilliantly, the hot red and yellow annuals among the vegetables and the herbaceous perennials carrying colour through August – as does the inventively planted annual border with its castor oil plants, grasses and *Verbena bonariensis*: no Victorian bedding plants here. In September the colchicum meadow is at its best, and an autumn border has been developed using late herbaceous perennials mixed with grasses. There's always something new at Cambo, and it's on a high with the buzz of success about it. *SGS, Good Gardens Guide.*

The house: This is a Victorian mansion in the grand style, with staff. Magnificent and luxurious are the bedrooms; the yellow room was once used for servicing the dining room, which is more of a banqueting hall – you breakfast here in the summer months. You are welcome to view this, and also the first-floor billiard room and drawing room. There is a delightful sitting room for your use on the ground floor overlooking the fountain. If you B&B in one of the studio apartments for two, Garden (with double) and Orchard (with twin), both with lovely parkland views, you may come and go as you please.

Price	£90–£130. Singles £47–£65.
Rooms	3 + 2: 2 four-posters (1 with separate bath/shower); 1 twin/double (let with four-poster). 2 B&B or self-catering studios, each for 2.
Meals	Dinner from £45. Pub 1 mile.
Closed	Christmas & New Year.
Directions	A917 to Crail, through Kingsbarns. Follow signs for Cambo Gardens, follow drive to house.

Sir Peter & Lady Erskine
Cambo House, Kingsbarns,
St Andrews KY16 8QD

Tel	01333 450054
Fax	01333 450987
Email	cambo@camboestate.com
Web	www.camboestate.com

 Travel Club Offer. See page 290.

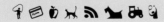

Entry 119   Map 9

18 Queen's Terrace

The garden: A super surprise awaits you here: fragrance and structure are the key themes to Jill's hidden water garden. On warm days you can enjoy a slow breakfast on the south-facing deck as finches, long-tailed tits and collared doves sing away in the cherry tree. An old brick path winds through terraced beds of silver and pink planting: astrantias, old shrub roses and herb geraniums. You will be lulled by the sound of water gently cascading from the ponds into the rill, fringed by arum lilies, ferns and primulas. Jill's creative flair is evident throughout: sculptures, unusual seating areas and quirky finds from the seashore. The path leads on down past a charming summer house and raised beds of herbs, vegetables and cut flowers; the scents are such a treat everywhere. Not content with just gardening her own patch, Jill and a couple of friends took on the creation and planting of 90 tubs and 85 hanging baskets for St Andrews in Bloom, and won 'Best Coastal Town' in Scotland – very impressive! This is a wonderful garden in which to chase the sun and Jill is happy to let you wander at will: just to find a quiet spot and bask; whatever the season you will find something to delight the senses.

The house: So peaceful it is hard to imagine that you're in the heart of St Andrews and a mere ten-minute walk from the Royal & Ancient golf club. Jill's stylish and traditional home shows off her artistic flair; the light, restful drawing room and elegant dining room are full of character, sunlight and flowers. Large bedrooms have especially comfortable beds, crisp linens, whisky and water, and poetry and prose on bedside tables. An enchanting place – and Jill, friendly and generous, is a mine of information on art, gardens and walks; sit on the terrace in summer and admire the water garden.

Price	From £85. Singles £65-£70.
Rooms	4: 3 doubles, 1 twin.
Meals	Dinner, 3 courses with wine, £20-£35.
Closed	Rarely.
Directions	Into St Andrews on A917; pass Old Course Hotel. Right at 2nd mini r'bout, left through arch at 2nd mini r'bout. 250 yds, right into Queens Gardens. Right at T-junc. On left opp. church.

Jill Hardie
18 Queen's Terrace,
St Andrews KY16 9QF

Tel	01334 478849
Fax	01334 470283
Email	stay@18queensterrace.com
Web	www.18queensterrace.com

Entry 120   Map 9

Inverugie

The garden: The garden is imbued with family history – Lucy's family has been here for 70 years. Sixty years ago the entire walled garden – one and a half acres, double-tiered and reached via a bluebelled woodland walk – was dug up by soldiers who planted potatoes for the war. Lucy's grandmother later rescued it with the help of one of the gardeners who helped to create the BBC Beechgrove garden in Aberdeen. Now the top third is a resplendent fruit and vegetable garden with heavenly views. Below, lawns, shrubs and trees, and a wide stone path weaving its way around box hedges, bee pond (happy bees!) and curved rose and herbaceous borders. The bottom section of the garden has a 'yellow' garden and another gorgeous rose garden; many of the roses were bred up here with creative input from Lucy's grandmother. Although her garden areas are distinct, Lucy has allowed scope for spontaneity and whim: euphorbia, hosta, alchemolis and meconopsis are dotted throughout, and the little garden house brings on jasmine and pelagoniums in spring that are transferred to the house in early summer. Inverugie is surrounded by 30 stunning acres: rolling fields, ancient protected woodland and a cup and ring standing stone dating from 3000BC. No wonder Lucy is passionate about it all.

The house: A handsome Georgian house with lofty porticos, generous bays, tall windows and impressive drive. The feel is solid and traditional inside: velvet sofas in sage-green and rose, floral curtains at pelmetted windows, touches of Art Deco... toile de Jouy in the double, cream padded headboards and new beds in the twin. The large dining and drawing rooms look over ancient woodland, pasture land and grazing sheep; beyond, beaches, castles, standing stones and rivers rich with salmon and trout. Lucy is a dynamo, finding time for riding, field sports, three young children and you; she even grinds her own flour for your bread.

Price	£60-£70.
Rooms	2: 1 twin/double; 1 double with separate bath.
Meals	Dinner £25. Pub 1 mile.
Closed	Christmas & New Year.
Directions	To Forres on A96, through Kinloss on B9089 to College of Roseisle village & over B9013. Veer right (for Duffus) & 1.3 miles on, left to Keam Farm. Past farm, house at end of road through stone pillars.

Lucy Mackenzie
Inverugie,
Hopeman IV30 5YB

Tel	01343 830253
Email	machadodorp@compuserve.com
Web	www.inverugiehouse.co.uk

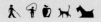 Travel Club Offer. See page 290.

Ethical Collection: Food.
See page 294.

Nether Swanshiel

The garden: Shiel (or shieling) means 'summer grazing', a name still apt in this fertile and deeply rural area. Originally built around 1760, Nether Swanshiel is one of four houses in the tiny hamlet of Hobkirk. When the Aulds arrived in 1996 their one-acre garden was a wilderness, but they set to, cutting back undergrowth and thinning trees, and opening up the views towards Bonchester Hill and down the river to the church. Gradually the original structure re-emerged; this now forms the basis for their own creation. The garden and house talk to each other through the new terrace, and a herbaceous border around the retaining wall supplies the house with the fresh flowers that Sylvia loves to have in the rooms. The Aulds are keen members of the Henry Doubleday Research Association, and their organic methods are reaping rewards: the garden is alive with birds and an ever-increasing population of bees and butterflies. Old-fashioned yellow azaleas scent the spring, wild orchids flourish under the fruit trees in the wild corner, and martagon lilies pop up in unexpected places. This is a tranquil place for both wildlife and visitors: a recently acquired paddock has meant the addition of a goat, Jacob sheep, hens and two geese. *HDRA, Friend of Royal Botanic Garden, Edinburgh.*

The house: In gorgeous, unspoilt border country this listed Georgian manse is handy for all points north and an easy drive away from Edinburgh. Sylvia, a smallholder, is a thoughtful hostess and excellent cook: Aga-baked scones or gingerbread for tea, organic produce when possible for dinner, and a choice of good things (kippers, proper porridge, corn fritters, compotes, homemade bread) for breakfast. Eat by the Victorian bay window overlooking the terrace in the cosy guest sitting room with a log fire. Sleep deeply in very private rooms, simply and softly furnished, with good beds; you will only hear sheep.

Price	£70. Single £35.
Rooms	3: 2 twins, each with separate bathroom; 1 single sharing bath (let to same party only).
Meals	Dinner £20 (if staying min. 2 nights). Village pub 1 mile.
Closed	November–February.
Directions	B6357 or B6088 to Bonchester Bridge. Turn opposite pub (Horse & Hound). Beyond church 1st lane to right. Set back off road.

Dr Sylvia Auld
Nether Swanshiel, Hobkirk,
Bonchester Bridge TD9 8JU

Tel	01450 860636
Fax	01450 860636
Email	auld@swanshiel.wanadoo.co.uk
Web	www.netherswanshiel.fsnet.co.uk

 Travel Club Offer. See page 290.

Entry 122   Map 9

You should find your hosts well-informed about gardens and nurseries in their areas. However, the details of the following organisations and publications may be of help when planning a trip. Publications are in italics.

The National Trust

Britain's premier conservation charity looks after the largest and most important collection of historic gardens and cultivated plants in the world. Over 200 gardens and landscape parks encompassing over 400 years of history are open to the public throughout England, Wales and Northern Ireland. They employ more than 450 skilled gardeners and thousands more volunteers.

The National Trust Handbook, listing all Trust properties open to the public, is available at £9.50 from the Trust's own shops, good bookshops and from the National Trust.

PO Box 39, Warrington,
Cheshire WA5 7WD
Tel: 0844 800 1895
www.nationaltrust.org.uk
enquiries@thenationaltrust.org.uk

The National Trust for Scotland

The conservation charity that protects and promotes Scotland's natural and cultural heritage for present and future generations to enjoy. The annual *National Trust for Scotland Guide* features more than 128 properties in its care, and costs £5 inc. postage.

Wemyss House, 28 Charlotte Square,
Edinburgh EH2 4ET
Tel: 0844 49321000
Fax: 0844 493 2102
www.nts.org.uk
information@nts.org.uk

The National Gardens Scheme

The famous *Yellow Book.* A guide to over 3,500 gardens in England and Wales, the majority of which are not normally open to the public. Divided by county, this invaluable book briefly describes the gardens and lists the days on which they open for charity.

Hatchlands Park, East Clandon,
Guildford, Surrey GU4 7RT
Tel: 01483 211535
Fax: 01483 211537
www.ngs.org.uk
ngs@ngs.org.uk

Scotland's Gardens Scheme

Scotland's own *Yellow Book* features around 350 private gardens north of the border that are not normally open to the public but which open their gates for charity on certain dates. *Gardens of Scotland,* an annual handbook, is available from 1 February each year, and full details of the gardens will also appear on the website.

42a Castle Street,
Edinburgh EH2 3BN
Tel: 0131 226 3714
www.gardensofscotland.org
info@sgsgardens.co.uk

The Royal Horticultural Society (RHS)

Since its foundation in 1804, the Royal Horticultural Society has grown to be the UK's leading garden charity. It promotes gardens and good gardening practices through its inspirational flower shows, and over 1,000 lectures and demonstrations. Its four flagship gardens are Wisley in Surrey, Rosemoor in Devon, Hyde Hall in Essex, and Harlow Carr in North Yorkshire. The Society has also joined forces with over 120 partner gardens in the UK and Europe that offer free access to its members. Among the RHS's many publications, the following are very useful:

The RHS Garden Finder by Charles Quest-Ritson (Think Publishing Ltd) and *The RHS Plant Finder* (Dorling Kindersley), both £14.99.

80 Vincent Square,
London SW1P 2PE
Tel: 0845 260 5000
www.rhs.org.uk
info@rhs.org.uk

National Council for the Conservation of Plants and Gardens (NCCPG)

The NCCPG seeks to conserve, document, promote and make available Britain and Ireland's great biodiversity of garden plants for the benefit of horticulture, education and science. An independent charity, it has 40 local groups supporting its aims through their membership and their propagation and plant sales. These efforts, together with the dedication and enthusiasm of National Plant Collection™ Holders, enable the NCCPG to fulfil its mission to conserve the vast gene pool of plants cultivated within the British Isles. *The NCCPG Directory*, listing over 660 National Plant Collections, is available at £6.50 inc. p&p.

12 Home Farm, Loseley Park,
Guildford GU3 1HS
Tel: 01483 447540
Fax: 01483 458933
www.nccpg.com
info@nccpg.org.uk

Henry Doubleday Research Association (HDRA)

The HDRA is Europe's largest organic membership organisation dedicated to researching and promoting organic gardening, farming and food. The Association has three organic display gardens open to the public, at Ryton near Coventry, Yalding near Maidstone in

Photo: Barn Close, entry 19

Kent, and Audley End near Saffron Walden in Suffolk. On two weekends a year, some HDRA members open their gardens to the public.

Garden Organic Ryton,
Coventry CV8 3LG
Tel: 024 7630 3517
Fax: 024 7663 9229
www.gardenorganic.org.uk
enquiry@hdra.org.uk

Hardy Plant Society (HPS)

The Hardy Plant Society was formed to foster interest in hardy herbaceous plants. With about 10,000 members and over 40 groups in England, Scotland and Wales, the Society aims to provide information about the wealth of both well- and lesser-known plants, and to ensure that all worthy plants remain in cultivation and have the widest possible distribution. The HPS organises study days and residential weekends, and publishes an annual seed list offering over 2,500 varieties, many unobtainable commercially.

Pam Adams, The Administrator,
Little Orchard, Great Comberton,
Pershore, Worcestershire WR10 3DP
Tel: 01386 710317
Fax: 01386 710117
www.hardy-plant.org.uk
admin@hardy-plant.org.uk

Cottage Garden Society (CGS)

The CGS was founded in 1982 when many 'old-fashioned' plants were becoming unavailable commercially. Now there are 45 groups, and approximately 6,000 members worldwide, and cottage garden flowers have become more readily available. The CGS continues to help its members find plants that are only produced in a few specialist nurseries, and gives them

Photo: Tom Germain

the opportunity to find 'treasures' through its annual Seed Exchange.

Clive Lane, Administrator, 'Brandon',
Ravenshall, Betley, Cheshire CW3 9BH
Tel: 01270 820940
www.thecgs.org.uk
clive_lane_cgs@hotmail.com

Alpine Garden Society (AGS)

With 14,000 members, the AGS is one of the largest specialist garden societies in the world. Founded in 1929, it promotes interest in alpine and rock garden plants, including small plants and hardy perennials, many bulbs and ferns, hardy orchids, and dwarf trees and shrubs, encouraging their cultivation in rock gardens and conservation in the wild. The AGS has a show garden at Pershore, and organises worldwide tours to see plants in their natural habitats.

AGS Centre, Avon Bank,
Pershore, Worcestershire WR10 3JP
Tel: 01386 554790
Fax: 01386 554801
www.alpinegardensociety.net
ags@alpinegardensociety.net

Herb Society

The UK's leading society for increasing the understanding, use and appreciation of herbs and their benefits to health. It has its headquarters at the delightful and historic Sulgrave Manor, which dates from 1539 and was once the home of George Washington's ancestors. The Society has created two herb gardens

there, one of which received an RHS Silver Medal award at Chelsea.

Sulgrave Manor, Sulgrave,
Nr Banbury, Oxfordshire OX17 2SD
Tel: 01295 768899
Fax: 01295 768069
www.herbsociety.co.uk
info@herbsociety.org.uk

Plantlife International

Britain's only membership charity dedicated exclusively to conserving all forms of plant life in its natural habitat.

14 Rollestone Street,
Salisbury, Wiltshire SP1 1DX
Tel: 01722 342730
Fax: 01722 329035
www.plantlife.org.uk
enquiries@plantlife.org.uk

Garden History Society

The Society's threefold aims are firstly to promote the study of the history of gardening, landscape gardening and horticulture; secondly to promote the protection and conservation of historic parks, gardens and designed landscapes, and to advise on their restoration; and thirdly, to promote the creation of new parks, gardens and designed landscapes.

70 Cowcross Street,
London EC1M 6EJ
Tel: 020 7608 2409
Fax: 020 7490 2974
www.gardenhistorysociety.org
enquiries@gardenhistorysociety.org

The Association of Gardens Trusts

This national organisation represents the growing number of County Garden Trusts whose main aim is to assist in the protection, conservation, restoration or creation of garden land in the UK for the education and enjoyment of the public.

70 Cowcross Street,
London EC1M 6EJ
Tel/fax: 020 7251 2610
www.gardenstrusts.org.uk
agt@gardenstrusts.org.uk

The Historic Gardens Foundation

A non-profit-making organisation set up in 1995 to create links between everyone concerned with the preservation, restoration and management of historic parks and gardens. Its *Historic Gardens Review* is published twice a year and offers lively and authoritative coverage of historic gardens worldwide. Members also receive three newsletters annually.

34 River Court, Upper Ground,
London SE1 9PE
Tel: 020 7633 9165
Fax: 020 7401 7072
www.historicgardens.org
office@historicgardens.org

Museum of Garden History

The world's first Museum of Garden History was founded in 1977 at the restored church of St Mary-at-Lambeth next to Lambeth Palace, the London residence of the Archbishop of Canterbury, just across the Thames from the Houses of Parliament. The Museum's unique collection tells the story of the history of gardening and the work of celebrated gardeners. Special focus is given to the Tradescant family who were gardeners to Charles I and Charles II. Plants first introduced to Britain by the Tradescants in the 17th century feature in the Museum's garden, as does the Tradescant family tomb. Open Tuesday to Sunday 10.30am–5pm.

Lambeth Palace Road,
London SE1 7LB
Tel: 020 7401 8865
Fax: 020 7401 8869
www.museumgardenhistory.org
info@museumgardenhistory.org

Border Lines

Border Lines takes select groups to outstanding private gardens in the UK, including many that are not open to the general public. Three gardens are visited on each day tour, and the party is shown around by the owner, designer or head gardener. Refreshments include a two-course lunch with wine, and there is also an opportunity to buy plants. A gorgeous day out.

James Bolton,
Clapton Manor, Clapton-on-the-Hill,
Cheltenham, Gloucestershire, GL54 2LG
Tel: 01451 821804
www.border-lines.co.uk
james@jamesboltongardentours.co.uk

PLANT HERITAGE

NCCPG

The National Plant Collections®

Protecting the nation's plant heritage

Conservation through Cultivation

The National Council for the Conservation of Plants and Gardens is the largest charity solely devoted to the conservation of plants by growing them in gardens.

Prior to 1978, the UK was at risk of losing some of its most precious and historic cultivated plants due to disease, fashion, complacency and the pressures of commerce.

Now, 660 National Plant Collections are held within the Scheme, securing around 80,000 plants, many of which are endangered.

By joining the network of local groups you can support the work of the Collection Holders and benefit from an active plant exchange, attend lectures, garden visits and specialist plant sales.

Please JOIN US (£25 for a single member) and help continue this important conservation work.

NCCPG Directory 2009 Published every Spring price £5.00 (+ postage). Includes all National Plant Collections and open days.

NCCPG
12 Home Farm,
Loseley Park,
Guildford,
Surrey GU3 1HS

Tel: 01483 447540
Fax: 01483 458933
Website: www.nccpg.com

Becoming a member of Sawday's Travel Club opens up hundreds of discounts, treats and other offers at many of our Special Places to Stay in Britain and Ireland, as well as promotions on Sawday's books and other goodies.

Where you see the 🧳 symbol in this book it means the place has a special offer for Club members. It may be money off your room price, a glass of champagne or a garden tour. The offers for each place are listed on the following pages. These were correct at the time of going to print, but owners reserve the right to change the listed offer. Latest offers for all places can be found on our website, www.sawdays.co.uk.

Membership is only £25 per year. To see membership extras and to register visit www.sawdays.co.uk/members. You can also call 01275 395433 to set up a direct debit.

The small print
You must mention that you are a Travel Club member when booking, and confirm that the offer is available. Your Travel Club card must be shown on arrival to claim the offer. Sawday's Travel Club cards are not transferable. If two cardholders share a room they can only claim the offer once. Offers for Sawday's Travel Club members are subject to availability. Alastair Sawday Publishing cannot accept any responsibility if places fail to honour offers; neither can we accept responsibility if a place changes hands and drops out of the Travel Club.

England
Bath & N.E. Somerset
2   10% off stays Monday-Thursday.

Bristol
4   Bottle of wine on arrival – hopefully to drink in the idyllic garden.

Buckinghamshire
5   One half-price evening meal, or taxi to destination in Milton Keynes area.
6   Fruit/vegetables from the garden or jar of homemade jelly. 10% off stays Monday-Thursday.
7   Wine with dinner.

Cheshire
9   Glass of champagne on arrival.

Cornwall

16   Cornish fare. Luxury toiletries.

Derbyshire

22   Afternoon cream tea and cakes, bottle of wine in your room, for stays of 2+ nights.
25   2nd night free on 2-night stays; dinner must be booked and paid for on one evening.
26   10% off mid-week stays. Earlier check-in by arrangement.
30   10% off stays Monday-Thursday or bottle of wine with dinner.
31   Late checkout.
32   Aperitif of choice before dinner. Bottle of wine for stays of 4+ nights. 5% off 2nd and subsequent stays.

Gloucestershire

37   Drinks tray in sitting room. Selection of DVDs in bedrooms.
38   10% off stays of 3+ nights, November-April.

Herefordshire

41   Bottle of wine or chocolates if celebrating a birthday, honeymoon or anniversary.
42   One voucher per room per night to a designated garden within 20 miles of Brobury. Valid for 5 days. Regular change of garden.
45   4th night free on 4-night stays Monday-Thursday.
46   Glass of champagne on arrival. Teenagers stay for half price.

Isle of Wight

49   Late checkout (12pm). Bottle of house wine.

Lincolnshire

56   Home-grown produce, as in season and available.

London

58   Tea/coffee with homemade cake/biscuits on arrival.
59   Jar of house preserve in room. Pick-up from local station. Bottle of house wine with dinner.
60   Free-range eggs on departure. Tea & coffee when staying all day (by arrangement).

Northamptonshire

65   Garden tour for plant lovers. Advice on propagation, growing, pruning. Seedlings when available.

Oxfordshire

67   5% off stays Monday-Thursday.

Shropshire

72   10% off room price Monday-Thursday. Wine and chocolates in fridge for stays of 2+ nights.

74   10% off stays Sunday-Thursday.

Somerset

75   Pick-up from Castle Cary train station. House cocktail per person per night and 15% off room price for stays of 2+ nights, Monday-Thursday.

76   Afternoon tea.

77   Tour of vineyard and (when available) glass of wine.

80   Pick-up from Dunster stations, drink per person per night, jar of Exmoor honey and 1/2 dozen free-range eggs (when available).

Suffolk

83   10% off stays Monday-Thursday, except during August and the Aldeburgh Festival.

Sussex

86   Tea and cake on arrival. Pick-up from local pubs or stations.

88   Glass of wine and selection of canapés at 6pm each evening of visit.

89   One plant, when available, per room for stays of 2+ nights Sunday-Thursday.

90   15% off 2-night stays Monday-Thursday (not mid-May to September).

91   10% off stays Monday-Thursday. Bottle of wine in room.

Warwickshire

94   Pick-up from Warwick Parkway station. 10% discount for members of Armed Forces.

96   10% off stays Monday-Thursday.

98   A plant propagated from the garden: tree, shrub or herbaceous (wide range to choose from).

103   Pick-up from local train station. Cuttings upon request.

105   2 plants of your choice from our nursery.

Wales
Powys

111   Organic bottle of wine. 10% off stays for repeat guests.

Scotland

Angus

113 One free supper for stays of 3+ nights (November-May).

Argyll & Bute

115 3 nights for the price of 2.

Edinburgh & the Lothians

117 Reduction of £10 per room for 4+ nights (except August). Glass of wine pre-dinner or night cap. Local history tour.

Fife

119 10% off stays of 2+ nights Monday-Thursday.

Moray

121 Bottle of wine with dinner.

Scottish Borders

122 Organic home produce.

Photo: Rock Farm House, entry 53

Many of you may want to stay in environmentally friendly places. You may be passionate about local, organic or home-grown food. Or perhaps you want to know that the place you are staying in contributes to the community? To help you we have launched our Ethical Collection, so you can find the right place to stay and also discover how each owner is addressing these issues.

The Collection is made up of places going the extra mile, and taking the steps that most people have not yet taken, in one or more of the following areas:

• **Environment** Those making great efforts to reduce the environmental impact of their Special Place. We expect more than energy-saving light bulbs

Photo: Broniwan, entry 109

and recycling – in this part of the Collection you will find owners who make their own natural cleaning products, properties with solar hot water and biomass boilers, the odd green roof and a good measure of green elbow grease.

• **Community** Given to owners who use their property to play a positive role in their local and wider community. For example, by making a contribution from every guest's bill to a local fund, or running pond-dipping courses for local school children on their farm.

• **Food** Awarded to owners who make a real effort to source local or organic food, or to grow their own. We look for those who have gone out of their way to strike up relationships with local producers or to seek out organic suppliers. It is easier for an owner on a farm to produce their own eggs than for someone in the middle of a city, so we take this into account.

How it works

To become part of our Ethical Collection owners choose whether to apply in one, two or all three categories, and fill in a detailed questionnaire asking demanding questions about their activities in the chosen areas. You can download a full list of the questions at sawdays.co.uk/about_us/ethical_collection/faq

We then review each questionnaire carefully before deciding whether or not to give the award(s). The final decision is subjective; it is based not only on whether an owner ticks 'yes' to a question but also on the detailed explanation that accompanies each 'yes' or 'no' answer. For example, an owner who has tried as hard as possible to install solar water-heating panels, but has failed because of strict conservation planning laws, will be given some credit for their effort (as long as they are doing other things in this area).

We have tried to be as rigorous as possible and have made sure the questions are demanding. We have not checked out the claims of owners before making our decisions, but we do trust them to be honest. We are only human, as are they, so please let us know if you think we have made any mistakes.

The Ethical Collection is a new initiative for us, and we'd love to know what you think about it – email us at ethicalcollection@sawdays.co.uk or write to us. And remember that because this is a new scheme some owners have not yet completed their questionnaires – we're sure other places in the guide are working just as hard in these areas, but we don't yet know the full details.

Ethical Collection in this book

On the entry page of all places in the Collection we show which awards have been given.

A list of the places in our Ethical Collection is shown below, by entry number.

Environment
42 • 69 • 89 • 99 • 111

Community
8 • 66 • 78 • 88 • 89 • 93 • 99 • 104 • 117

Food
8 • 27 • 42• 52• 66 • 68 • 69 • 74 • 80 • 88 • 89 • 98 • 99 • 104 • 107 • 111 • 121

Ethical Collection online

There is stacks more information on our website, www.sawdays.co.uk. You can read the answers each owner has given to our Ethical Collection questionnaire and get a more detailed idea of what they are doing in each area. You can also search for properties that have awards.

Photo: Grey Lodge, entry 1

Quick reference indices

Stay all day
Guests can stay all day if
they wish.

Produce
Produce grown and sold here.

Evening meals
Evening meals available;
book in advance.

Quick reference indices

Quick reference indices

Travel without a car
Within 10 miles of a bus/coach/train station and owner can arrange collection.

The National Cycle Network
These places are within 2 miles of the National Cycle Network

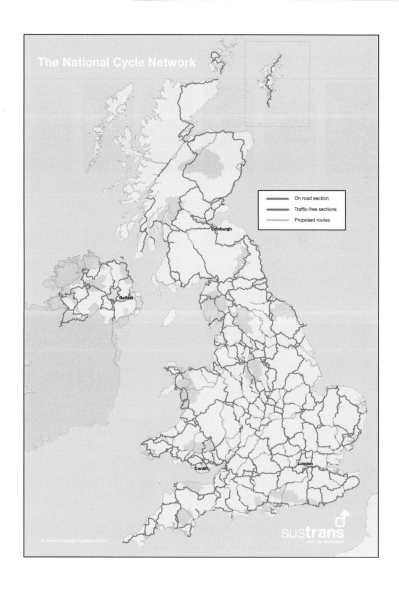

Have you enjoyed this book? Why not try one of the others in the Special Places to Stay series and get 35% discount on the RRP *

British Bed & Breakfast (Ed 13)	RRP £14.99	Offer price £9.75
British Bed & Breakfast for Garden Lovers (Ed 5)	RRP £14.99	Offer price £9.75
British Hotels & Inns (Ed 10)	RRP £14.99	Offer price £9.75
Devon & Cornwall (Ed 1)	RRP £ 9.99	Offer price £6.50
Scotland (Ed 1)	RRP £ 9.99	Offer price £6.50
Pubs & Inns of England & Wales (Ed 5)	RRP £14.99	Offer price £9.75
Ireland (Ed 7)	RRP £12.99	Offer price £8.45
French Bed & Breakfast (Ed 11)	RRP £15.99	Offer price £10.40
French Holiday Homes (Ed 4)	RRP £14.99	Offer price £9.75
French Hotels & Châteaux (Ed 5)	RRP £14.99	Offer price £9.75
Paris Hotels (Ed 6)	RRP £10.99	Offer price £7.15
Italy (Ed 5)	RRP £14.99	Offer price £9.75
Spain (Ed 7)	RRP £14.99	Offer price £9.75
Portugal (Ed 4)	RRP £11.99	Offer price £7.80
Croatia (Ed 1)	RRP £11.99	Offer price £7.80
Greece (Ed 1)	RRP £11.99	Offer price £7.80
India (Ed 2)	RRP £11.99	Offer price £7.80
Green Places to Stay (Ed 1)	RRP £13.99	Offer price £9.10
Go Slow England	RRP £19.99	Offer price £13.00

*postage and packing is added to each order

To order at the Reader's Discount price simply phone 01275 395431 and quote 'Reader Discount GBB'.

If you have any comments on entries in this guide, please tell us. If you have a favourite place or a new discovery, please let us know about it. You can return this form or visit www.sawdays.co.uk.

Existing entry

Property name: _____

Entry number: _____ Date of visit: _____

New recommendation

Property name: _____

Address: _____

_____

Tel/Email/Web: _____

Your comments

What did you like (or dislike) about this place? Were the people friendly? What was the location like? What sort of food did they serve?

_____

_____

_____

_____

_____

Your details

Name: _____

Address: _____

_____

_____ Postcode: _____

Tel: _____ Email: _____

Please send completed form to:
GBB, Sawday's, The Old Farmyard, Yanley Lane, Long Ashton, Bristol BS41 9LR, UK

Photo: South Lodge, entry 5

(1) The Yat

(2) Powys

(3) The garden: In a supreme setting of rolling hills studded with sheep is the Yat: a listed house dating from the 15th century, with logs piled in the porch and swallows dipping in and out. The sloping terraces around the house are thought to date from Elizabethan times; the remains of flagstone paths can be detected still. Years ago Krystyna and Derek fell in love with these eight acres, where nature predominates and the only sounds you hear are birdsong and whispering wind. The first thing they did was plant trees on the steep slopes to the sides. Now there are 1,000 – mostly deciduous, some coniferous – providing shelter for plants and a wonderful haven for wildlife. The ancient terraces were extended in the south-facing part of the garden, retained by ivy-straggled stone walls and reached by stone steps. The garden, an on-going project, is a mixture of formal and wild: of blackcurrant bushes and wild strawberry plants that have merrily self-seeded, of tiered organic vegetable gardens and topiary. Pass the overgrown pond down the lane to the ruins of a baptistry and a tiny patch of burial ground. Or sit by the fountain that trickles over the little cast-iron boy with swans, and hear the doves coo. There's a sense of timelessness to this place: in Krystyna's words, "a unity of mind, man and nature".

The house: Come for stunning scenery, a characterful household and an engaging hostess. The listed house, once the home of the wicked squire of Bevan, has hung on to its ancient flags and beams; the feel, thanks to charming artist Krystyna, is one of calm, and there are many beautiful things to look at. Bedrooms are quaint, bathrooms plain with special touches (white robes, good soaps) and there's space to roam: a sitting room, a conservatory, a snug library with games. Food is almost all organic, breakfasts and suppers scrumptious and local. This is a grand place to really rest and recharge your batteries.

Price	£75. Singles from £55.
Rooms	2: 1 double, 1 twin.
Meals	Dinner, 3 courses, £30 (incl. glass of wine, coffee & biscuits).
Closed	Rarely.
Directions	Directions from Hundred House village: road to Glascwm, signed at crossroads; at next T-junc., left over hump-backed bridge; left at next junction; 1st house on right.

Krystyna Zaremba
The Yat, Glascwm,
Llandrindod Wells LD1 5SE
Tel   01982 570339
Fax   01982 551032
Email   krystyna.zaremba@theyat.net
Web   www.theyat.net

Travel Club Offer. See page 290.

Ethical Collection: Environment; Food. See page 294.

Entry 111   Map 2

---

(4) Price   £75. Singles from £55.

(5) Rooms   2: 1 double, 1 twin.

(6) Meals   Dinner, 3 courses, £30 (incl. glass of wine, coffee & biscuits).

(7) Closed   Rarely.

(8) Directions   Directions from Hundred House village: road to Glascwm, signed at crossroads; at next T-junc., left over hump-backed bridge; left at next junction; 1st house on right.

Krystyna Zaremba
The Yat, Glascwm,
Llandrindod Wells LD1 5SE
Tel   01982 570339
Fax   01982 551032
Email   krystyna.zaremba@theyat.net
Web   www.theyat.net

(9) Travel Club Offer. See page 290.

(10) Ethical Collection: Environment; Food. See page 294.

(12)

(11) Entry 111   Map 2